Through a careful look at some of Jesus's most challenging conversations, Chase helps us better understand the trap of offense and how Jesus can rescue us from it. Like a skilled surgeon, Chase uses Jesus's words to dissect our lives, helping us recognize the insecurity and idolatry that often leads us to envy and offense. Jesus loves us enough to be honest with us. For those willing to listen, his hardest words also turn out to be some of his best. With Chase's usual mix of history, psychology, and literature, *A Sharp Compassion* is a fascinating and sober read. For those willing to take the journey, you'll learn and certainly be changed.

MARK BATTERSON, lead pastor of National Community Church; New York Times bestselling author of *The Circle Maker*

Good therapists know how to be warm, compassionate, and empathetic. But they also know when to be challenging and confrontive if that preferred approach is not working. Jesus was a good therapist. And Chase Repogle is also a good clinical theologian, and an engaging writer. In this wonderfully transparent book, he examines some of Jesus's own words of "sharp compassion" to help the reader find a more examined and free way to live, and to love.

GARY W. MOON, M.Div., Ph.D., Founding Executive Director Martin Institute and Dallas Willard Center, and current director of *Conversatio Divina*, at Westmont College and author of *Apprenticeship with Jesus,* and *Becoming Dallas Willard.*

In our desperate search for comfort, the temptation to minimize, neutralize, or distort the cross looms large for Christians navigating the fragility of our own shortcomings. But the cross is offensive. As Chase Replogle reminds us, 'the cross is the singular offense we must not lose, for it frees us from all other offenses.' *A Sharp Compassion* is a timely diagnosis of our contemporary condition, offering a challenging but accessible, difficult but beautiful path forward, away from suffocating fragility, toward a spacious and free life.

JAY Y. KIM, Pastor and Author

The most powerful writings serve as a catalyst for change. This book is one of those that packs the potential to transform the reader. Chase inspires all of us to take an introspective look at our desires, our insecurities, our relationships, our ability to imitate Jesus, and even our view of Christ's Cross. This book propelled me to consider ways I can choose to be blind to what Jesus wants to reveal in me or I can embrace offense as a mechanism to uncover the work Jesus longs to do in my heart and life. Ultimately, this book empowered me to consider every offense—or temptation to be offended—as an opportunity to intentionally take my eyes off myself and place my gaze solely on Jesus allowing nothing to replace him in my heart and life. This powerful book will certainly shift your perspective and approach to offense and deepen your understanding of Jesus!

SHONNA CRAWFORD, PhD, Convoy of Hope, Vice President, Convoy:Women

In a highly polarized society, it can seem like most Christians either feel a moral obligation to cause offense as often as possible (especially online), or are convinced that any offense is automatically unbiblical and wrong. In *A Sharp Compassion*, Chase Replogle finds the biblical thread that doesn't let either side off the hook but brings the offense of the gospel into a sharper, more Christlike focus.

KARL VATERS, author of *De-sizing the Church*, Founder of *Helping Small Churches Thrive* at KarlVaters.com

In his earthly ministry, Jesus sometimes offended people. He never intended to demean or denigrate, however. Instead, as my pastor Chase Replogle points out in *A Sharp Compassion*, Jesus' words were surgical, aimed at healing sin-sick souls. We become better when we take His words to heart. Chase takes you deeper than the obvious, unpacking the spiritual warfare involved and equipping the reader with tools that are practical yet deeply seeped/rooted in theological, psychological, and sociological substance. The content is truly life changing!

DONNA BARRETT, General Secretary of the Assemblies of God

The self-absorbed tendencies of 21st century western Christianity have served to domesticate Jesus and make him an inoffensive means of achieving our own selfish ends. Yet the call of Jesus that blesses us also confronts and offends us. Here Chase shines as a writer, thinker, and pastor. He deals with the hard sayings of Jesus in a way that leave us both convicted and stronger. His treatment of our battles with insecurity, idolatry, and imitation are particularly brilliant. Read this book ready to do some deep heart work.

JAMES BRADOFRD, PhD, Lead Pastor, Central Assembly, Springfield, MO

Leaders know too often the dangers of offense and envy, and Chase shines a new light on the topic and helps us break free from its trap. This book unpacks some of Jesus's most difficult truths with a fresh perspective. Take to heart the words of Jesus—read this book and learn its lessons!

BRAD LOMENICK, Leadership consultant, speaker, founder of BLINC, and author of *The Catalyst Leader* and *H3 Leadership*

The best writers help us take a second look at what we thought we knew. Chase is one of those writers. Surveying our current landscape of 24-7 outrage, Chase leverages the words of Jesus to help us see not only that our proclivity to offense says more about us than it does about whatever the issue du jour may be, he also helps us see just how the resurrected Christ may be speaking to us in our offense, healing our sin-sick souls, leading us to freedom. A book to be pondered and prayed over.

ANDREW ARNDT, Lead Pastor, New Life East. Author, *Streams in the Wasteland: Finding Spiritual Renewal with the Desert Fathers and Mothers*

A Sharp Compassion is a needed and timely word for today. By unpacking Jesus' encounters with others, Chase leads the reader down a path that demands introspection. In a world where we go out of our way to be politically correct, this book will show you that Biblical correction is not only necessary - it's something to be grateful for.

LAUREN VANDER LADEN, author of *I Want to Move On*

A SHARP COMPASSION

7 Hard Words to Heal Our Insecurities
and Free Us from Offense

CHASE REPLOGLE

A Desk and And A Dog

Edited by Andrew J. Spencer, Paul W. Smith, and Blake Atwood
Interior design: Chase Replogle
Cover design: Chase Replogle
Cover image: Copyright © 2023 S&K Byzantine Icons
Author photo: Jessica Yates

ISBN: 979-8-9908732-1-6 (eBook)
ISBN: 979-8-9908732-0-9 (Paperback)

A Desk & A Dog is an independent publisher focused on creating books that integrate faith, culture, and the great conversations. For more information on other books (and resources) created from a biblical perspective, go to www.adeskandadog.com or write to:

A Desk & A Dog
5517 N Farmer Brach Rd #101
Ozark, MO 65721

For my daughter, Charlotte

May Christ's words, even those hardest to receive, always serve to free you from this world of insecurity, envy, and offense.

— Dad

TABLE OF CONTENTS

The wounded surgeon plies the steel
That questions the distempered part;
Beneath the bleeding hands we feel
The sharp compassion of the healer's art
Resolving the enigma of the fever chart

Our only health is the disease
If we obey the dying nurse
Whose constant care is not to please
But to remind of our, and Adam's curse,
And that, to be restored, our sickness
  must grow worse.

— T.S. Eliot, *Four Quartets*

CHAPTER 1

HARD WORDS TO HEAR

"He who dares not offend cannot be honest."

THOMAS PAINE

"It is funny how mortals always picture us as putting things into their minds: in reality our best work is done by keeping things out."

C.S. LEWIS, THE SCREWTAPE LETTERS[1]

"**S**ee that guy over there?" I whispered, pointing to a man standing near the altar. "I work with him. He got fired this week."

"For what?" my friend whispered back.

"Poor job performance, I guess. I don't know all the details, but I heard they walked him out to his car."

Before he was fired, we had worked together on staff at the church, a large congregation with a coffee shop, fitness center, and newly installed theater seating. We were in different departments, and I didn't know him well. I was only a Bible college student working part-time at the church. I couldn't believe I'd been hired. In a matter of weeks, I had gone from visiting the church for the first time to sitting in on staff meetings and participating in important decisions.

But sitting there ready to worship, what had motivated me to bring up such a distracting thing? At the time, I couldn't have told you. Who thinks about motives when some bit of gossip works its way to your tongue? You speak and think later, if at all. Like most indiscretions, our real motivations are usually somewhere beyond our awareness. As Edward Bernays, the nephew of Freud, explained, "Men are rarely aware of the real reasons which motivate their actions."[2] We live unaware of the forces at work in our inner lives.

Who knows why people do what they do? We make mistakes. We call it sin, shrug, repent, and move on. On Sunday, the pastor reminds us of the doctrine of total depravity. We hear it not as a warning but as an explanation, even an absolution. The complexity of sin at work within us rarely inspires us to dig deeper. It feels too tedious. These days, too much talk about sin makes you sound prudish, morbid, even fanatical. We may not have it together, but we know people far worse. The human heart is totally depraved and, in my experience, totally uninterested in it.

We have no trouble recognizing the reality of sin in our world. We see it clearly in each day's news of more violence, chaos, and hatred. We recognize it in the annoying habits and wounding actions of neighbors, coworkers, and family. We are experts at recognizing everything that is wrong with our world, but how rarely do we find a reason to turn that same critical eye of investigation toward our own hearts and inner lives? We know what is wrong with the world and yet know very little about what is truly wrong with ourselves.

The Bible warns that sin is far more than bad behavior. God explained in the opening pages of Genesis, "Sin is crouching at the door. Its desire is contrary to you, but you must rule over it."[3] Sin is hiding and waiting to defeat you. It is not only in your actions but lurking in your heart. You must learn to see it, or you will be ruined by it.

Sin is a trap, a snare, baited and hidden to cause your fall. Enticed into that trap, you are most vulnerable when you are least suspicious of it. The smell of the bait draws you in with the promise of fulfillment and pleasure. Eventually, that disinterest comes with a cost. The snare is tripped; you find yourself caught. The more you struggle, the more the snare tightens. If you've ever had a sin exposed, you know what I'm describing. You thrash and roll, blame and accuse. But you can't get free.

I want to show you how sin works: how the trap is baited, how the hidden snare is set, and the consequences of overlooking it. But be prepared; it often takes a hard word to get your attention and free you from the snare. And the same word required to free you risks offending you. The most dangerous animal is always the one that feels trapped. Corner a snared animal and you're likely to get bit even if you seek to free it. As you sense the trap closing, you become irrational, prone to suspicion, and less likely to recognize your salvation. You reject the very word meant to set you free. But if you learn to see the trap, you'll also learn to recognize God's hard word as one of rescue.

* * *

Fatigued from a recent hip injury, C. S. Lewis overslept and missed his regular 8 a.m. service at Holy Trinity Church. He usually arrived at the service late enough to avoid the opening hymns, which he referred to as "fifth-rate poems set to sixth-rate music."[4] But Lewis had missed several weeks and, waking up late, decided to attend the midday service instead. There in his regular pew by the stone column, bored by the sermon (as he often was), Lewis was struck by an idea. He later wrote to his brother:

> Before the service was over—one could wish these things came more seasonably—I was struck by an idea for a book which I think might be both useful and entertaining. It would be called *As One Devil to Another* and would consist of letters from an elderly retired devil to a young devil who has just started work on his first 'patient.' The idea would be to give all the psychology of temptation from the other point of view.[5]

Lewis wrote that book and titled it *The Screwtape Letters*. The book contains a collection of letters from a senior tempter to his novice nephew with instructions on tempting his young human patient away from God. I remember first reading the book as a teenager and being struck by the depth of Lewis's understanding of human temptation and the blindness of the human heart.

What makes *The Screwtape Letters* so fascinating is the complexity of temptation orchestrated beneath the "patient's" awareness, a central theme of the book. The two tempters scheme tactics for drawing the young man away from any consciousness of their work. Secrecy and subversion are their stock in trade. But, after revealing himself to his patient, the young tempter loses him to the Christian faith. His uncle replies, "How well I know what happened at the instant when they snatched him from you! There was a sudden clearing of his eyes (was there not?) as he saw you for the first time, and recognized the part you had had in him and knew that you had it no longer."[6]

Recognizing what's happening in your heart is more than half the battle of overcoming sin. But recognizing it is no easy task. It's one for which all hell and your own polluted condition plot to thwart.

In your heart resides the whole of history. In your heart stirs the story of sin and idolatry, the fall of man, and humanity's rebellion against God. In your heart plays out the dramatic tale of rebellion, repression, and redemption. All of it is there. All of heaven and hell crammed into that small cavity of your chest, and yet you pass most days with no more awareness of that cauldron brewing within you than you are aware of the churning molten rock at our planet's core. If reading *The Screwtape Letters* accomplishes anything, it opens your eyes to just how much is at work within you. There is more going on in your heart than you have recognized.

> How shrewd Screwtape was to recommend that his apprentice aggravate that most useful human characteristic, the horror and neglect of the obvious. You must bring him to a condition in which he can practice self-examination for an hour without discovering any of those facts about himself which are perfectly clear to anyone who has ever lived in the same house with him or worked in the same office.[7]

The Old Testament prophet Jeremiah understood it too, writing, "The heart is deceitful above all things, and desperately sick; who can understand it?"[8] We can't understand it on our own. Introspection often uncovers very little.

How, with so much distraction and temptation stacked against us, can anyone ever understand their own inner life? The Bible and believers throughout history have long recognized an important tool for learning to see within your own heart. It is not easy nor without risk, but for the hardest of hearts, it often takes a strong blow. Christ comes to reveal what you most need, to split open your heart, and to expose what is true. He will be honest with you about your real condition.

David McCracken, Professor Emeritus of English at the University of Washington, has written extensively on offense in culture, literature, and, specifically, the Bible. He explains that it is the "difficult-to-bear, personal nature of an offense, its confrontational nature that makes it hard to ignore or to shrug off, its blatant attack on what we take to be our deepest selves or our strongest allegiances—these are precisely what give the offense its power. The offense has a way of bringing the individual to a moment of crisis, revealing the heart's desire."

But many are unwilling to hear that word. How few are those who have ears to hear? So it is that many are offended by Jesus. What we need is a deeper understanding of offense and how Jesus wields offense for his purposes. From the old French *offendre*, to offend simply means to strike, to cut, to wound. Offense is a sword. And that risk of offense, those cutting, piercing words of Jesus, are often just what we need to break through the slab of our indifference.

God himself will risk offending you to save you.

* * *

To be clear, as I gossiped about that coworker, I was not thinking about sin or my motivations. I certainly wasn't thinking about the doctrine of total depravity or any trap. But just as that service was about to begin, I was unexpectedly forced to take a long, hard, uncomfortable look at what had motivated my words. It came as a word of offense.

My motivation for gossiping may not have been clear to me, but there was at least one person to whom it was perfectly clear. I've always whispered too loudly, but to my surprise, the woman seated in front of me turned around. Red in the face, she let me have it.

"You should be ashamed of yourself," she said, her voice shaking with anger. "You work at this church and speak about your brother like that. You don't even know what you're talking about. You have no business saying what you're saying, and you have no business working here if that's how you treat people. Something is wrong with you, not him."

If she had waited and confronted me after service, if she had just begun with a simple, "Pardon me, I couldn't help but overhear—," I might have been capable of mounting some kind of self-justification, as pathetic as it probably would have been. But something about the intensity of her correction caught me entirely off guard. There was, for a very small moment, that rising feeling of offense. That upward rushing sense of indignation. *Who was she to speak to me like that? She didn't even know me.*

But I could not answer. The worship team struck their first chord, and the service began. I stood there, humiliated and ashamed. I was sick with it. I hadn't seen it coming. I realized at that moment things were stirring in me to which I had given no real attention. My careless words had been more than gossip. But that was only a symptom of something far worse at work inside.

I realized she was right. They were hard words, but they were true. Often, the truest words are the hardest to hear. But they're often just what we most need.

* * *

I want to suggest something to you that will sound both strange and possibly offensive, especially given our cultural moment. But I am convinced it is true—convinced by both my past experiences and by the consistent witness of Scripture. If you are willing to endure being offended and honestly look at it, what offends you can reveal important characteristics about you. Offense can be a form of revelation. It can shock you into seeing things you've overlooked about yourself. Understanding what offends you can even lead you to a deeper faith in Christ. But it will require a willingness to confront Christ's hard words and not be offended by them.

I still think about that Sunday service and that woman's confronting words. To this day, I do not know who she was, nor have I ever spoken to her again. If I ever met her, I would only want to tell her thanks. I am grateful for what she did. She could have waited to discuss it with her husband on the drive home. She could have gossiped about me to someone else in the church. She could have said nothing at all. But instead, she risked offending me and, in the process, helped save me from the dark and destructive forces I was blind to in my own heart. She made me see something I needed to see.

Once I was forced to see it, it didn't take much work to connect all the pieces. I had turned that new job at an influential mega-church into an idol. I imagined it validated me. Seeing a coworker's failure gave me some meager feeling of superiority. I was in; he was out. It was a cheap trick to sedate my own insecurity. What a distorted thing to hold in your heart. How dangerous to act without knowing it was there.

Who knows what your heart holds? Who knows what is there even now, neatly concealed and desperately avoided?

But while offense can be a powerful tool for breaking through your heart's defenses, offense can also be your excuse for avoiding the vulnerability of that introspection. That is the perplexing reality of offense. Offense can reveal, but it can also harden your defenses.

REVELATION OR SUPPRESSION

I recently saw a man at Walmart with a sweatshirt that read "I'm offended that you're offended." That sentiment feels accurate for our time. These days, who isn't offended? You can hardly turn on the television or scroll social media without hearing someone claiming to be offended. Every day, another public figure is forced to apologize to "anyone they may have offended." Offense has become so common the internet now has a whole genre of "I'm offended" memes. Offending or being offended seem constantly at the center of our conversations about everything from politics to art to business to comedy and, certainly, religion. The world is wound tighter, the stakes higher, and everyone seems anxious, annoyed, and offended.

In an interesting set of dual statistics, the Pew Research Center found that 53 percent of adults in the United States now believe "people saying offensive things" is a major problem in our country. However, that stat is complicated by 65 percent who believe "people being too easily offended" is the major problem.[9] That means a significant margin of people must believe both statements are true—there is too much offense, and people are too easily offended by it.

Another way to observe the trend is the frequency with which we now claim offense. Google's database of more than 129 million digitized books can be easily searched for changes in how we use words and phrases. Called the Ngram Viewer, it charts phrases on a line graph to display their frequency across time. The tool can reveal patterns in usage as far back as the 1500s. Search the phrase "I'm offended" and the resulting trend line is striking.[10] Up until about 1950, the phrase was used sparingly. You can see its gradual growth throughout the late-1900s. But beginning around 2000, the frequency line makes an almost vertical climb. This century, the phrase "I'm offended" has grown in usage by more than 5,600 percent. In 2016, The Collins English Dictionary named the term "snowflake generation" one of its words of the year. The phrase describes an entire generation's tendency to take offense easily.[11] Perhaps people have always felt offended, but we certainly seem to be talking more about it.

No previous age has given as much attention to offense, but we aren't making much progress in reducing it. Instead, we're growing more divided, and our conflicts only seem to make us more sensitive to it. Each offense drives new wedges and fragments our society more deeply. The more we're offended the more we contribute to the offending.

We can't even agree on whether offense is actually a problem. Some seem determined to double down on offense, offending to prove a broader point about our culture's sensitivities. Others resolve to show no offense at all and so abandon all distinctions for the sake of vague affirmations and some naively hoped-for agreeableness. What few seem to be doing is asking why. Why are we increasingly sensitive to offense, and why can't we control it? Perhaps we find being offended easier than the alternative: being honest about its cause.

Offense can be revelation, but it can also be a tactic of suppression. Offense is an easy way to avoid facing what is in our own hearts. When a hard word threatens you externally, the last thing you want to acknowledge is that it might be right and that you might be blind to it. You claim offense, partly as a strategy to shield your vulnerability.

The language of offense allows you to object to the threat without the liability of explaining why it hurt so deeply. Claiming to be offended grants you the moral high ground. It is a tactic of defense, just as a king is willing to tear down his whole city to reinforce the walls before an invasion. Offense often hardens the defenses of your heart and focuses your attention on the external threat at the cost of self-awareness. It allows you to respond with outrage rather than despair.

Political cartoonist Tim Kreider explains,

> Obviously, some part of us loves feeling 1) right and 2) wronged. But outrage is like a lot of other things that feel good but, over time, devour us from the inside out. Except it's even more insidious than most vices because we don't even consciously acknowledge it's a pleasure. We prefer to think of it as a disagreeable but fundamentally healthy reaction to negative stimuli, like pain or nausea, rather than admit that it's a shameful kick we eagerly indulge again and again.[12]

Being offended is addicting, in part because it shields us from our own sin and insecurity. But it's a dangerous trick. The more you feel offended, the more you feel justified in it, and the less you care to know why. As you give into the impulse, you become increasingly less aware of the internal mechanisms fueling it. As a result, you become less capable of understanding your own inner life and motivations. Offense always begets more offense. Embracing offense moves you further into the darkness. It makes you less self-aware.

It's a strange paradox, but the more we stumble over the same obstacle of offense, the less willing we are to acknowledge it's there. What offends us becomes an obsession. It's not hard to see this fixation in the way offense has swept through our culture, hijacked our public conversations, and absorbed our private thoughts. French thinker René Girard described offense as "not one of those ordinary obstacles that we avoid easily after we run into it the first time, but a paradoxical obstacle that is almost impossible to avoid: the more this obstacle, or scandal, repels us, the more it attracts us."[13] Few will admit it, but we can become addicted to offense. That addiction makes it increasingly difficult to see our own vulnerabilities.

Jesus recognized that offense would be an unavoidable part of the human experience. He warned his own disciples, "It is impossible that no offenses should come."[14] Jesus knows we will face offense. But the real question is, will we be blinded by it, caught up in its obscuring obsession, or will we look honestly at what it reveals? Can we recognize offense as an opportunity? Offense will either lead to revelation or suppression. It depends on how we respond. And how we respond to offense will also shape how we hear the words of Christ. Jesus did not shy away from offending. Instead, he recognized that the truest word often risks offending us.

JESUS AND OFFENSE

In 2020, as the world spiraled downward into political division, vaccine debates, and church fractures, our congregation decided to focus on Jesus. Honestly, I was naively trying to avoid all the conflict and the constant pressure to weigh in on each week's new developing controversy. Instead, we took our time in the gospel of John and tried to stay calm in the presence of Jesus. For that year, we spent each Sunday working verse by verse through the fourth gospel, grounding ourselves in Christ and his words.

What's better for calm and tranquility than Jesus? Jesus in some peaceful pasture. Jesus welcoming a group of kids. Jesus walking a dusty road with his disciples, the sun setting over the gentle tides of Galilee. It's the old image of Jesus and those footprints in the sand.

> *Gentle Jesus, meek and mild,*
> *look upon a little child,*
> *pity my simplicity,*
> *suffer me to come to thee.*[15]

That's a prayer for children, but it's an image most of us have held on to. We like to imagine Jesus above all the conflict and offense. We like to imagine him somehow serenely detached from it. We retreat to Jesus to get away from all that offends. What we rarely imagine is what the Gospels actually record, that when people met Jesus, they often left offended by him.

Offense constantly surrounded Jesus's ministry. And far from avoiding it, Jesus even seemed to provoke it. Jesus had to remind his own followers, "Blessed is he who is not offended because of me."[16] As, David McCracken writes in *The Scandal of the Gospels*, "If we assume that Jesus is a kind, gentle, and loving hero and that such traits are antithetical to offensiveness, we as readers will do whatever we can to ameliorate any apparent offensiveness in the text."[17] And that is largely what we have done.

Perhaps we're willing to accept a version of Jesus that offends the same people we enjoy offending. Sure, Jesus occasionally came down hard on those self-righteous Pharisees, but what no one likes to imagine is Jesus offending them. No one expects to open the Bible and find Jesus coming down hard on them. But if you remove the offense of Jesus's words, you risk robbing them of their power.

Jesus offended his disciples, even those closest to him. He offended the crowds. He offended his own family and his hometown.

He offended Jews and gentiles, rich and poor, male and female, political leaders, and religious teachers. Peter and Paul both went so far as to label Jesus a stone that causes stumbling.[18] They called Jesus an offense and pointed out that preaching the gospel would cause others to be offended as well.

I had turned to the gospel of John to try and avoid offense. Instead, I kept finding conversations full of it. I came across a phrase by the Danish philosopher Søren Kierkegaard that captured my experience in John's gospel. Kierkegaard described conversations with Jesus as "frightful collisions."[19]

Those conversations of offense forced me to reconsider what offense was and why it was so common in Jesus's ministry. It forced me to listen, reckon with hard words, and search my own heart. And I discovered that while many walked away from Jesus due to offense, others found in those same words a breakthrough of faith. They encountered real offense and yet found their eyes opened, their hearts exposed, and their souls moved to believe. When Jesus risked offense, some walked away and others pressed in. Some were blinded by it and others found new sight. Jesus's hardest words are a key component of his good news.

I'm not suggesting we rework Jesus into a swaggering, cursing, ill-tempered brawler, as some have attempted to do. We can't put words in Jesus's mouth, but neither should we take them away. The temptation is to try and make Jesus just one thing. We must instead do the much harder work of holding together both images of Christ. He is peaceful, loving, gentle, and lowly, and he is also confrontational, frank, and sharp with rebuke.

G.K. Chesterton described the true believer's ability to hold together these two images:

He has always cared more for truth than for consistency. If he saw two truths that seemed to contradict each other, he would take the two truths and the contradiction along with them. His spiritual sight is stereoscopic, like his physical sight: he sees two different pictures at once and yet sees all the better for that.[20]

Our ability to hold on to these two pictures of Jesus preserves his real depth. Think of it this way: You technically see two distinct images of every object. The space between your eyes means each eye has a slightly different angle of the world. Your brain fits those two images together into a single image, giving you a greater perception of depth and movement. Two unique images merge into a single vision of the world's forms and contours. Losing one eye can cause a significant loss in depth perception, the perception of movement, and your ability to judge distances. So, too, having only one image of Christ can jeopardize your ability to perceive his real depth and movement. Without both views, Christ collapses into a one-dimensional preference.

Again, Kierkegaard provides helpful in his warning of a diminished Christ. Kierkegaard wrote to a Danish Christian culture that gave little attention to the actual Christ, having assumed that their Danish identity certified their Christian faith. Kierkegaard recognized that in polite Danish society, Jesus's message had been simplified and emptied of its offense. It had been watered down to make it palatable to that culture and so lost its power.

"Take away the possibility of offense, as they have done in Christendom," Kierkegaard wrote, "and the whole of Christianity is direct communication; and then Christianity is done away with, for it has become an easy thing, a superficial something which neither wounds nor heals profoundly enough; it is the false invention of human sympathy which forgets the infinite qualitative difference between God and man."[21] Kierkegaard warned of a faith built on one-way communication. We worship but make no room for God to convict. We talk of God but have lost our ear for hearing his voice. We have opinions about God but care very little for his opinion of us. Only a Christ, Kierkegaard contended, who is permitted to risk offending can cut deeply enough to heal.

That idea is foreign to modern faith. We are looking for affirmation and power, not conviction and correction. But Jesus is willing to tell us the truth. As the book of Hebrews describes it, he wields a two-edged sword that cuts deep enough to reveal the secrets of the heart, mind, soul, and spirit.[22]

In the book of Revelation, that two-edged sword emerges from his mouth, judging what is true from what is false.[23] His sword is his word, dividing, rebuking, correcting, and revealing. If you come near Christ, if you listen, he will reveal what is in your heart. But only you can decide if that truth will humble you or blind you with offense.

Like antiseptic in a wound, being saved is not always comfortable. Stitches, lances, and reset bones never feel good, but they are the work of healing. The physician must sometimes cut deeply to abstract what ills. So, too, offense is often the heat of Christ's light shone into our deepest needs, his greatest work done within those secret places of your deepest vulnerabilities.

It is just as the old man Simeon saw it, lifting the newborn child in the temple and prophesying, "This child is destined to cause the falling and rising of many in Israel, and to be a sign that will be spoken against, so that the thoughts of many hearts will be revealed."[24] Simeon got it right. Many did stumble over Jesus. Many fell and went away offended. But others found what Simeon also saw: their hearts revealed and their faith formed. When you truly encounter Christ's word in all of its dimensions, it will offend you or it will cure you. The outcome is up to you.

UNCOVERING THE MECHANISM OF OFFENSE

Jesus does not seek to offend. But he will not let our sensitivity to offense keep him from telling us the truth. His hardest conversations are our guide to understanding the trap of offense and learning to receive from even those hard words. What lies ahead in this book is a view beneath the surface of offense. I want to use Jesus's conversations to help us explore beneath the controversy, beneath the headlines, beneath the memes, the outrage, and the trends.

Have you ever seen one of those Rube Goldberg contraptions? A ball rolls down a track and releases a rope that runs through a pulley and raises a board that flips a switch that finally turns on a light. Goldberg was a cartoonist who liked to draw absurdly complex mechanical processes for achieving simple tasks. To understand them, you had to follow the machine one step at a time. As a kid, we used to play a board game called Mouse Trap that involved one of those complicated Rube Goldberg machines. The contraption would run—crank, boot, bucket, ball, slide, catapult—until, eventually, the plastic net came down on the mice beneath. Your heart is a similar Rube Goldberg machine. As we uncover the mechanisms of offense, you'll find it depends on a similarly complex series of linked feelings, assumptions, and desires that play out in your heart.

In the following chapters, we'll look more closely at how that machine of offense works. You'll learn to recognize how each step triggers a response: how an obstacle forms in your insecurity, which draws you to an image, which triggers an imitation, which demands affirmation, and which finally provokes accusation and unleashes offense.

Every offense is an opportunity to break the progress of the machine. Expose it and you can keep from being snared by it. But to recognize it, you must be willing to look hard at your own heart and to listen closely to Jesus's actual words, even when they risk offending. Jesus's hard conversations will help you finally recognize the trap of offense.

I didn't write this book to offend you, but I do hope it leads you into a moment of crisis, the kind of crisis that strips away the superficial and allows you to sense again those things that matter most. I hope it reveals your heart's desires and insecurities, and I hope this book will enable you to better understand the mechanisms at work in your heart. I hope you come to recognize and appreciate the good but sometimes hard words of Jesus. They are, as C. S. Lewis described them, a "severe mercy,"[25] or, in the words of T. S. Eliot, a "sharp compassion."[26]

* * *

"My son, do not regard lightly the discipline of the Lord,
nor be weary when reproved by him.
For the Lord disciplines the one he loves,
and chastises every son whom he receives."
Hebrews 12:5–6

CHAPTER 2

OFFENSE: "GET BEHIND ME, SATAN!"

"Get behind me, Satan! You are a stumbling block to me; you do not have in mind the concerns of God, but merely human concerns."

MATTHEW 16:23, NIV

"The true way goes over a rope which is not stretched at any great length but just above the ground. It seems more designed to make people stumble than to be walked upon."

FRANZ KAFKA[1]

The Gospels do not tell us why Jesus took his disciples north, but it was there, somewhere beneath the snowcapped peak of Mount Hermon, along the cold spring water feeding the upper Jordan, that Peter had a revelation. Jesus turned to his disciples and asked, "Who do people say that I, the Son of Man, am?"[2] They repeated what they had heard, everything from Elijah to John the Baptist. Jesus then asked, "Who do you say that I am?"[3] If any of them had thought it, none had yet risked saying it out loud. But characteristically bold, Peter said what others could not, "You are the Christ, the Son of the living God."[4]

Perhaps Peter himself did not fully understand what he had confessed, for Jesus added, "Flesh and blood has not revealed this to you, but my Father who is in heaven."[5] Peter had said more than he realized. Jesus added it would be upon that rock that he would build his church. It was a definitive moment in Jesus's ministry and certainly in Peter's life. It must have built Peter's confidence, for he soon spoke again with even greater boldness.

As they went on, Jesus described what it would mean for him to be the Messiah. He would have to suffer, be rejected, and ultimately die—a stark contrast to the swelling popularity they had experienced in Galilee. The crowds had been growing, his message had been spreading, and miracles were breaking out. Jesus's sudden interest in rejection must have seemed strangely out of place. At that apparently high spiritual moment, Jesus's talk of suffering didn't sit well with Peter. He didn't do it publicly, but Peter found an opportunity to pull Jesus aside, and, as Scripture says, Peter rebuked Jesus. "Stop talking like that," Peter corrected. "This suffering will not happen to you. God forbid it."[6]

Peter's rebuke was firm, but I've always imagined it in a low whisper, a correction meant to be quiet and tactful. He might even have thought he was bolstering Jesus's faith, but Jesus did not respond with Peter's discretion. Instead, Jesus turned quickly and spoke to Peter with a severity unmatched in the Gospels: "Get behind me, Satan! You are a stumbling block to me; you do not have in mind the concerns of God, but merely human concerns."[7] Peter must have staggered backward at such an unexpected blow. How could he have just spoken words revealed by God and now be speaking for Satan?

Peter was one of Jesus's first followers and one of his closest friends. How unexpected it was that Jesus would speak his harshest criticism to his closest disciple. Did Jesus snap? Did he lose his cool with their continued misunderstanding? Did the pressure of what lay ahead finally get to him? Couldn't he have reminded Peter of the resurrection and how it would all be okay in the end? Wasn't this just a misunderstanding? Didn't Jesus know Peter's heart?

For Peter and the rest of the disciples, Jesus's talk of suffering was the most difficult to comprehend. They could recognize Jesus's power, his authority, and even his identity as the Messiah, but they could not make sense of his predicting rejection and suffering. Their image of a messiah was one of uncompromising success. They couldn't understand why he diluted it with talk of defeat.

But Jesus recognized what Peter could not. Jesus saw what we are prone to overlook as well. It was much more than a misunderstanding. Peter may have realized who Jesus was, but his desires were blinding him to what Jesus had to do. Peter had slipped into the logic of Satan.

French writer Simone Weil observed that evil never feels like evil to those caught up in it. She wrote,

> Does not the evil that we do seem to be something simple and natural which compels us? Is not evil analogous to illusion? When we are the victims of an illusion we do not feel it to be an illusion but a reality. It is the same perhaps with evil. Evil when we are in its power is not felt as evil but as a necessity, or even a duty."[8]

Peter was caught in an illusion. What seemed so obviously true to him—the real possibility of their power, influence, and success—

was recognized by Jesus as a demonic temptation. Sometimes, the only way to break that kind of illusion is to be shocked back to reality. We must be startled into seeing it.

The southern novelist Flannery O'Connor often depicted shocking characters and situations in her stories for the same effect. She explained,

> When you can assume that your audience holds the same beliefs you do, you can relax a little and use more normal means of talking to it; when you have to assume that it does not, then you have to make your vision apparent by shock—to the hard of hearing you shout, and for the almost-blind you draw large and startling figures.[9]

So, Jesus spoke with staggering severity. Peter had made himself an obstacle in Jesus's path, an offense, and Jesus risked offending Peter to expose it. Jesus's response was strong precisely because he knew what lurked deep within Peter's heart.

* * *

In ancient Israel, a disciple usually selected their teacher. A person would voluntarily commit to a rabbi and begin following and imitating that teacher's life. Many followed Jesus under that model. They came to Jesus and took the initiative to follow him from place to place, listening and learning as they went.[10] But Jesus did not acquire his closest disciples that way. Instead, Jesus called particular individuals to follow him. Jesus's call to them came in the form of a radical command. Peter was one of the first. Seeing Peter casting his net into the sea, Jesus said to him, "Follow me."[11] It was not a request. It wasn't even an invitation. Jesus spoke it as a command. Some commentators have even described it as a demand.

Peter would have been familiar with the requirement of following a Jewish teacher. Jesus's command to follow was not figurative language. Jesus commanded Peter to leave his life and business and physically walk behind him: watching, listening, and learning. Jewish teachers did not attempt to teach by lectures alone. They offered their lives as a model. A disciple learned through imitation. They learned by observing and imitating that rabbi. To obey Jesus's command, Peter understood he would be reorienting his entire life to imitate Jesus. Peter dropped his nets, took up the call, and followed.

Jesus also gave Peter a new name. It had been Simon, an incredibly common name in the first-century Jewish world. But Jesus instead decided to call him Cephas or Peter, Petros in Greek.[12] Peter was not a common name. It meant rock, and Jesus offered it as a nickname. It also seems to have been aspirational.

From what the Gospels tell us, Peter was not always a rock. Jesus may have recognized his potential, but for much of the gospel story, Peter seemed unstable. He tended to speak without thinking, jump to conclusions, and assume he understood more than he usually did. At his best, he showed remarkable faith. At his worst, he fled in fear. Jesus frequently had to correct Peter and sometimes even ignored his bursts of exuberance.

The list of outbursts is long. When Peter witnessed Jesus transfigured on the mountain, Peter wanted to set up tents and stay. Jesus ignored him. When Jesus tried to wash his feet, Peter asked for his whole body to be washed, too. Jesus explained he was missing the point. When Jesus predicted Peter would deny him, Peter protested. When Jesus asked him to pray in the garden, Peter fell asleep. When the guards came to take Jesus away, Peter drew his sword and took off a man's ear. Jesus told Peter to put his sword away and healed the man.

Peter walked on water until he sank, confessed until he got it wrong, and followed until he denied even knowing Jesus. Whatever drew Jesus to Peter, he certainly wasn't a finished product. Yet Jesus wasn't afraid to keep working on him, chipping away at that rock of potential.

Jesus's call to discipleship always requires refinement. We follow so that we might be disciplined, reshaped, and formed. It was true of Peter and is also true for you and me. Why should we expect to get off better than Peter? If his closest disciple stumbled, do we expect always to get it right? And if Jesus was willing to rebuke him, why not us as well? Like Peter, our eyes drift. Our desires distort. We step out from behind Christ. We take up the logic of Satan. And by his grace, Jesus makes us see our mistakes. He saves us from ourselves. He calls us back into the position of following.

If you never find Jesus correcting you, is he really your teacher? Do you think you always get it right? When did Jesus last shock you into seeing something uncomfortable in your life? If you are following Jesus, you can be sure it will happen, and probably often.

Though Jesus's correction of Peter was short that day on the road north of Galilee, Jesus made a few very specific points. Jesus's first word was to force Peter back into a proper position of discipleship. "Get behind me," Jesus commanded. That was the position to which Peter had been called. "Follow me," Jesus had said. The Gospels are careful to include that Peter had taken Jesus aside. Peter led Jesus away from the other disciples. Peter was no longer behind his teacher. Before saying anything else, Jesus forced Peter back into the position of a disciple.

Next, Jesus located Peter's mistake not on some lapse of theological judgment but on Peter's fixation with the things of man. Peter's mistake was not a question of logic or a misunderstanding of ancient prophecy. Peter was driven by his longing for earthly things. The King James translation says Peter was savoring the things of man instead of the things of God. It is the language of desire. Peter was not thinking about God; he was thinking about himself, his expectations, and what he wanted. He did not want Jesus to suffer because he didn't want to suffer. Peter was no longer imitating Jesus; he was imitating the world. But that was not the worst of it.

In his rebuke, Jesus did not call him Peter, but Satan. He was no longer the rock upon which Christ was building; he had become the stone of offense, an obstacle in Jesus's path. Peter may not have realized it, but he was echoing the words and temptation of the demonic. Jesus recognized it immediately. He had heard it all before.

At the beginning of his ministry, Jesus was tempted by Satan in the wilderness. Satan used a very similar tactic. "Bend your knee," Satan suggested, "and I will just give it all to you."[13] He offered Jesus a path to power without the cross. He stepped in front of Jesus and offered a way out of the suffering, a new path, a detour. Jesus had answered Satan with a similarly fierce conviction, using the same words he would speak to Peter. Jesus commanded Satan to get behind him.

Satan also took Jesus up to the pinnacle of the temple and suggested he throw himself off of it. The angels would rescue him, and the nation would know Jesus's true identity, just as Peter would later confess it. To bolster his point, Satan offered Jesus the promise of Psalm 91: "On their hands they will bear you up, lest you strike your foot against a stone."[14] Given the context of Satanic temptation and the offer of world power, stumbling over a stone doesn't sound like a terrible danger. Is that what Jesus feared? Striking his foot on a rock? Scripture's promise was that Jesus wouldn't trip over a stone?

Jesus understood that image in a way that most of us have forgotten. And we continue to suffer the consequences for it. The Bible recognizes that one of the great tests we all face is the stone that lies in our path. Repeatedly, the Bible speaks of the rock that causes stumbling. And repeatedly, we are warned of being blind to it.

THE STONE OF OFFENSE

In the ancient world, where walking was the primary form of travel, stumbling was a very real and constant risk. With few paved roads and the rocky terrain of Israel, a traveler could stumble over plenty of obstacles. Out in the Judean wilderness, rolling your ankle on a rock or breaking your leg against a stone might even mean death. A stone in your path was a genuine danger, threatening your progress and safety. Every traveler was vulnerable to unseen obstacles.

Over time, the image of stumbling worked into the Jewish imagination and became a more significant symbol than the literal danger of tripping. In offering a blessing for those who live with wisdom and discretion, the book of Proverbs promises, "Then you will walk on your way securely, and your foot will not stumble."[15] The idea came to be a warning and a promise. You should be careful to avoid any obstacle which might lead to your fall and God alone can make the path of the righteous smooth and straight.

In both the Greek New Testament and the Greek Old Testament, the Septuagint, the word which describes these hidden obstacles was *skandalon*. From it, we get our English word scandal. The word rarely appears in Greek texts outside of the Bible, but the New Testament writers used it in its noun or verb form more than forty times. For context, that's as many times as the New Testament mentions salvation.[16] *Skandalon* is used by all four of the gospel writers and in the letters of Paul, Peter, and John. Biblical translators have long translated the word as "offense," recognizing in the image of stumbling over a hidden obstacle the similar experience of stumbling over an offense. It is the word *skandalon* which appears at the center of Jesus's rebuke of Peter: *Get behind me, Satan! You are a skandalon, an obstacle, a stumbling block, an offense.*

Peter made himself an obstacle to Jesus. Peter, the rock Jesus had been shaping into a disciple, became a stumbling stone in Jesus's path to the cross. It was physically true. Having moved from behind Jesus to standing in front of him, Peter blocked Jesus's way. But it was also spiritually true. Peter tempted Jesus to abandon the cross. He tempted Jesus to stumble. As Satan had done, Peter set himself up as an obstacle. Without recognizing it, Peter had participated in the ancient mechanism of temptation. He did the devil's work. He made himself an offense.

Given its frequent and prominent use in the biblical texts, why does the topic of offense so rarely come up in our Bible studies, sermons, or Christian books? My guess is this might be the first time you've read about offense as one of the major biblical themes. Why have we overlooked a topic so central to the teaching of Jesus and the reflections of his followers?

Part of the challenge is translation. Skandalon is used in very different contexts, and translating a word with such a wide range of usage poses a challenge for biblical scholars. While the King James Version often translates the word as "offense," most modern translations show no clear pattern. Skandalon is translated as "sin," "fall," "stumble," "obstacle," and even as generically as a "difficulty." The Revised Standard Version never uses the word offense at all. In *The Scandal of the Gospels*, McCracken points out, "With these varied translations, is it any wonder that we fail to recognize a common idea repeatedly surfacing?"[17] But perhaps there's an even more concerning reason.

René Girard suggested an additional problem. He believed our cultural sensitivity to offense had biased our reading toward weaker, lesser offensive words. Girard wrote, "Recent translators, trying to make the Bible psychoanalytically correct, attempt to eliminate all the terms censured by contemporary dogmatism."[18] Even if such decisions are unintentional, are we conscious of how our growing sensitivities are shaping our reading of the text? Girard feared such decisions have not only obscured the meaning of skandalon but have diminished the teaching of Jesus because of it.

McCracken also acknowledges how our sensitivity to offense has made translators, commentators, and pastors reluctant to recognize it. He wrote,

> Though there is no hiding all of the offense, we as readers are oblivious to much of it. It is regularly translated out, and interpreted out, of the Bible. And that is a scandal worthy of study, because without the offense a reader has a severe handicap when encountering ideas and characters of the Gospel, especially the hero, Jesus.[19]

How can we learn this lesson if we can no longer see it in our own Bibles?

Perhaps the most significant reason we've overlooked the

biblical theme of offense is our superficial understanding of how offense works and how serious it is. Writer Gil Bailie describes the biblical concept of offense as "the highly flammable mixture of envy, rivalry, jealousy, and resentment for which the word 'scandal' is a virtual synonym."[20] Offense is not just a human emotion, nor some category of sin; it is the mechanism by which our hearts are drawn into sin. It is a strategy used to cause our fall. It's a trap set to snare us. As such, the enemy seeks to shroud offense in secrecy and self-justifications. The Bible has long connected these obstacles of offense to our blindness. Failing to see them, we become trapped by them.

As a kid, my brother and I loved playing flashlight tag in the backyard. We would hide behind trees and bushes and attempt to run back to home base without being spotted by the flashlight. We had a great yard for the game with a large, wooded hill behind our house. Occasionally, we could even talk my parents into playing. My dad must have hidden deep in the woods at the top of the hill because we all heard him whooping as he sprinted down the slope in the darkness, determined to make it to the base at the center of our driveway. None of us remembered tying the rope between two of the trees earlier in the day. My dad discovered it. He hit it full speed at his knees and quickly found himself on the ground. No one dared call him out, though technically he was, as we rushed to him with our flashlights. He had been tripped by an obstacle he had not seen. To use the Bible's term, we had set up an offense. In the darkness, he was blind to it. He suffered its fall.

The Bible recognizes that the obstacles that trip us are often things we are blind to. Our vulnerability to offense is usually hidden from us. We trip because we don't recognize the obstacle. We fall because we have neglected to recognize our own vulnerabilities. We usually don't realize what's happened until we've hit the ground.

Do you see this blindness in Peter's rebuke of Jesus? Peter couldn't recognize that he had actually taken offense to Jesus's talk of suffering, and by it, he'd made himself an offense to Jesus. Peter stumbled over Jesus's talk of suffering and so set himself up as a stumbling block before Jesus. Jesus made Peter's mistake explicit, explaining that Peter was no longer dwelling on the things of God. He had taken his eyes off Jesus and become blind to how offense was misleading him.

You can take offense without recognizing that it is offense. You can stumble without recognizing what tripped you. We most often fail to recognize the source of our offense and our own blindness to it. As a result, the feeling of offense obscures its own root cause. Offense distracts us from itself. That's part of what makes offense so insidious and tempting. We take offense and give it, never realizing the logic of our real motives.

In the book of Leviticus, a very strange and specific prohibition is given against placing a stone in the path of a blind person, which might cause them to stumble and fall.[21] The Septuagint translators chose skandalon to describe that intentionally placed obstacle. Later, Jewish commentators were perplexed by the prohibition. Was this really a problem in the ancient world? Thou shalt not steal, kill, or trip blind people? Were Jewish youth running around tripping the visually impaired? Of course, the Old Testament includes a lot of detailed regulations, but even the ancient Jewish teachers wondered about this one.

The commentators began to interpret the rule as an allegorical warning against giving a vulnerable person false information or bad advice. They used the image to describe the many ways a person might be caused to fall into sin by ignorance or gullibility. That Levitical law was extended to things like predatory loan practices, selling goods that might lead to sin, and even neglecting to mark graves, lest a priest or pilgrim unknowingly wander over one and become unclean.[22] They saw these obstacles as traps. The blind risked falling into them. The Jewish teachers were especially concerned with any action or word that might become an obstacle to another person's pursuit of God, and they understood that it was our own spiritual blindness that made us most susceptible to these obstacles of offense.

Tripping us in our blindness and offending us where we are most vulnerable is exactly what Satan sets out to do. Theologian Robert Hamerton-Kelly concludes, "'Scandal' means the same as Satan."[23] Satan's goal is to cause our fall, and all the better if he can do it while keeping us blind to the obstacle we trip over. Satan loves to overthrow the human heart while offering it all kinds of self-justifications.

You may know that feeling of offense, but you may also struggle to see the real obstacle and to understand why you can't get past it. The only recognizable sign is your own frustration. You can't get what you want. You're never happy. It's never enough. And someone else is always to blame. You know how offense feels, but you know little about how it works. That's just where Satan places his obstacle. Between the trees in the dark. Right where you are most blind to it.

We are in grave danger. In our blindness, we sprint toward destruction. We trip but keep going, frustrated but still blind. And with every fall, we come closer to destruction. How can we be saved from what we can't even see?

Sometimes the only way to be saved is to be tripped before we fall. The biblical writers not only observed the obstacle of offense which leads to our destruction, but they also described the willingness of God to make himself an obstacle for our salvation. As Isaiah warned God's people, "He is the one you must respect; he is the one you must fear. He will become a sanctuary, but a stone that makes a person trip, and a rock that makes one stumble."[24] Though offense is the tactic of Satan, the Scriptures explain that God himself is willing to risk offending you to save you from Satan's obstacle.

RISKING OFFENSE TO EXPOSE IT

Before Eugene Peterson became a well-known pastor or writer, he was a teenage boy trying to work out his faith along the shores of Flathead Lake in Montana. Eugene's parents actively participated in ministry and church life, often welcoming missionaries and evangelists into their lakeside home. One summer, they hosted a well-known Pentecostal preacher. After some encouragement from his mother, Eugene finally approached the man with a question about his stagnant prayer life. It was the afternoon, and the seventy-year-old minister was lying in a hammock by the lake. Timidly, Eugene asked if the preacher might offer him some advice on prayer. Without opening his eyes, the minister grunted, "I haven't prayed in forty years!"[25]

Stunned, Eugene walked away, silent and confused. It was only much later he came to understand what had happened. "It took me about six or seven years to understand what he had done," Eugene would later write. "You see anything he had told me I would have imitated. I would have gone and done what he said and thought that's what prayer is. He risked something to teach me what prayer was, and I'm glad he did. Prayer wasn't something he did, it was something he was. He lived a life of prayer."[26]

I haven't tried this approach with any question from my congregation, but I think that old Pentecostal preacher recognized something important. Even with his eyes closed, he saw that folded into Eugene's question was an insecurity and a form of blind imitation that would keep Eugene's prayers from being his own. So, the evangelist risked being misunderstood to make a more important point. He made himself an obstacle to Eugene's pursuit, hoping to force the young man to reconsider his own desire and question. You might not like how he did it, and it might not be wise to repeat it, but that preacher's willingness to risk offense echoes a divine strategy.

Jesus, like that old minister in the hammock by the lake, understood that we need something more transformative than mere religious advice. Our condition of brokenness can't be solved with a better instruction manual. Hand us one and we're more likely to hold it upside down and start reading it backward. We're too blind even to take good advice. (Really, who reads instruction manuals?) We distort everything by our self-absorbed squinting. We're oblivious to most of the desires motivating our behavior and worship. We don't recognize what we really need. Like Peter, we are quick to speak, quick to assume, and ignorant to schemes of Satan stirring within even our best intentions. It's going to take more than a twenty-minute Sunday sermon and a thin paperback self-help book for us to get it.

Even as the crowds rushed to him, Jesus knew most were there for the bread and miracles. When he talked about consuming his body and blood, they took offense. John records that Jesus's own disciples were offended, and many walked away. When his disciples complained he had offended the Pharisees too, Jesus answered, "They are blind guides [of the blind]."[27] Jesus instead explained, "For judgment I have come into this world, so that the blind will see and those who see will become blind."[28]

Of course, none of us think we're blind. We see plenty. But often, what we see only blinds us further. How do you help a person recognize they are blind? Even now, as you read this, every part of you wants to assume I'm writing about someone else. None of us want to admit that Jesus's hardest words are for us. Perhaps there are other ways for this truth to break through, but certainly, one of the most effective is offense. An obstacle in your path trips you and, if you're willing, after brushing off the dust and regaining your composure, it can help you pay closer attention to the path you were on. Jesus often used such a tactic. He risked offending to help us recognize a much deeper need.

No one seeks God. No one understands. No one pursues righteousness. By his grace, God often makes himself an obstacle in our path. He trips us before our desires do, giving us a divine but sometimes painful moment of revelation, a chance to see the inner workings of our insecurities, and a chance to turn in faith toward him. It is as Dietrich Bonhoeffer encouraged, "We must be ready to allow ourselves to be interrupted by God. God will be constantly crossing our paths and canceling our plans."[29]

Before Christ is the way, he is an obstacle, the rope stretched taunt between the trees. He is the salvation that knocks us off our feet and breaks our stride toward destruction. This world does not need more offense. God forbid I contribute to it. But this world does need Christ. You need Christ. And Christ acknowledged that he would cause many to be offended. Knocked down by Jesus, we will either harden our offense or be transformed by it.

Each moment of offense is an opportunity. It may even be that God himself has orchestrated it. When you are offended, you must ask yourself a question: Might this be God allowing me to see what is in my heart? Might this be God rescuing me from coming destruction? You may find that the stone that first offended you is suddenly transformed into a foundation stone for an entirely new project.

THE OBSTACLE OR THE FOUNDATION

For all that Peter misjudged and got wrong, one profound characteristic saw him through. Peter accepted whatever Christ showed him. Peter was willing to see what Jesus exposed in him. In rebuke, in challenge, in the failure of his own denial, Peter returned to Jesus. And with time and still many more failures, Peter came to understand both Christ's suffering and his own call to likewise suffer. Church history records that Peter, when executed for his faith, requested to be crucified upside down, feeling unworthy to share in Christ's position. In the end, Peter chose to suffer as his final act of discipleship. He would follow Jesus even into his own death. Still, it may be in Peter's New Testament writings that we get the clearest picture of Peter's progress toward Christlikeness.

Peter described in Scripture how each of us must "come to him," Jesus, as our "living stone." Quoting from Isaiah, Peter merged two images. Jesus was the "stone of stumbling, and a rock of offense." Jesus was also the stone the builders rejected that had become the cornerstone. Peter, who must have understood those images in light of his own nickname, finally understood how Jesus was both a stone that caused our stumbling and a foundation stone upon which a new life and building were being built. [30]

As the first stone, the cornerstone gives shape to the building. Each stone that follows must be cut and adjusted to its lines. The first stone became the model for each stone added to the formation. Peter recognized how Isaiah's words gave language to his own experience of being reshaped by Christ. Peter bore the chiseled grooves of Christ's words reworking him into the shape of a true disciple. Some reject the blows of Christ's chisel and stumble over them. Others are reshaped to fit into Christ's foundation.

That is ultimately what it means for us to be disciples. We must allow ourselves to be reformed. We must allow the edges to be chiseled away, weaknesses fractured off. Our lives turned, tumbled, reworked, and reshaped into a form congruent with Christ's. The stacked stone has no say. Its shape is predetermined by that first stone of the foundation on which it is laid.

A willingness to receive the strong blows of God, necessary for reshaping your life, is not always easy. There is a constant temptation to be offended by each of those blows. There is a temptation to strike back or walk away offended. Only the true disciple is willing to recognize the blow for what it is: help and healing. Christ must do his work where we each need it most, in the depths of our own darkened hearts. We will either be offended or saved. The choice is yours.

* * *

Dante's *Divine Comedy*[31] is most often remembered for its strange depictions of the levels of hell, but the book makes an important point about the source of real change. Dante's story does not begin in hell. It begins with Dante lost in the woods. Dante is lost in darkness, blind to any path out of it. Afraid and disoriented, Dante comes across a light at the top of a mountain. He's determined to leave the dark woods and progress his life toward that elevated plane of light, but as he attempts to scale the mountain, he's stopped by three beasts: a leopard, a lion, and a wolf. They're obstacles.

Those animals have long been interpreted as the sins of lust, pride, and greed. Dante could not reach the light for his own sins, which blocked his progress, obstacles in his path. They threatened to devour him. And Dante did not have the means to overcome them. At that moment of frustration, the Greek poet Virgil appears and offers to guide Dante to the light. Dante agrees to follow, but Virgil leads him in an unexpected direction. Instead of climbing the mountain, Virgil guides him downward through the descending layers of hell. Level by level, Dante experiences the consequences and realities of sin. Like a cartographer mapping the contours of the inner life, Dante comes to understand how sin works and how to recognize his own.

Having reached the lowest level of hell, Dante and Virgil emerge unexpectedly on top of the mountain. The trajectory doesn't make physical sense. They descend into hell but somehow end up higher than they began. The point is not physical but spiritual. For Dante to grow in knowledge and progress toward God, he has to descend into the darkness of hell and his own heart. He has to overcome the obstacle by descending into it.

These obstacles are never random. To understand them, we need to go to the deepest part of our vulnerability. We need to go back to the beginning. Back to when God walked unobstructed in the cool of the garden with humanity. Back before any obstacle existed between us and God. Back before the serpent objected and awoke us to insecurity. If offense is a complex hidden trap in the heart, then the place in which we meet that obstacle is within. It is in your heart that the mechanism of offense begins to fire with its first spark of insecurity. You will always face offense at the place of your greatest insecurity.

* * *

"The way of the wicked is like deep darkness;
they do not know what makes them stumble." — Proverbs 4:19

CHAPTER 3

INSECURITY:
"WHY DO YOU CALL ME GOOD?"

"'Teacher, what good deed must I do to have eternal life?' And he said to him, 'Why do you ask me about what is good? There is only one who is good. If you would enter life, keep the commandments.' He said to him, 'Which ones?'"

MATTHEW 19:16–18

"We must allow the Word of God to confront us, to disturb our security, to undermine our complacency and to overthrow our patterns of thought and behavior."

JOHN STOTT

As Jesus entered the region of Judea, he was approached by a young man of great wealth and influence. Likely, he was the leader of the local synagogue. Perhaps it was his wealth that had helped him secure such a position of honor at such a young age, but the man did not lead with his wealth or even his respected role in society. He came to Jesus plagued by a personal question, and he spoke with what seemed to be a profound and heartfelt interest in spiritual things.

He had everything going for him: youth, wealth, position, and religiosity. Still, the young man threw himself at Jesus's feet, lifted his eyes, and asked, "Good Teacher, what must I do to inherit eternal life?"[1] For all he had achieved and possessed, you feel the weight of his question. He came to Jesus because he sensed there was something he still lacked. He came desperate.

Jesus had always responded positively to individuals who came in such postures of submission. He had healed many men who showed similar desperation. This young man falling at Jesus's feet had to be the opening of another decisive move of God, word of which would certainly spread throughout Judea. He asked a great question, and Jesus's disciples must have waited for a great answer.

Instead, Jesus replied coolly, "Why do you call me good?"[2] Jesus apparently wasn't so easily impressed. Bonhoeffer described Jesus's response as a "rude shock."[3] The offense came so abruptly that it seemed to cut the young man off. It was the first sign that their conversation would not go as the young man had expected nor as he had probably rehearsed. From that first word, the young man lost control of the conversation. He would not get it back.

Jesus did not follow the social script. His refusal to play the young man's game of pleasantries would certainly offend many today as well. Jesus's response risked coming across as rude in the face of the young man's talk of honor, but Jesus went on to place an even greater obstacle before him, one which the young man would soon stumble over. "Go, sell all that you have and give to the poor, and you will have treasure in heaven; and come, follow me."[4] The young man went away discouraged and grieved. Jesus created an obstacle he could not overcome. He left offended.

Between those two offenses—Jesus's interruption and Jesus's demand—there is a conversation worth giving close attention. The conversation does what Jesus's offense always does: it exposes the heart, and here, in particular, it exposes the insecurity at the young man's core. Though not immediately obvious, the young man's insecurity is ultimately exposed, along with his desperate fight to conceal it. Like most insecurity, it was not hard for others to see.

Word by word, Jesus revealed that things were not as they appeared. Religion can mask our insecurity. Service can disguise it. Wealth can guild it over with gold. But there is ultimately no coming to Jesus without acknowledging it. We are insecure.

To suggest such a thing may risk offending you, but that is only because insecurity is precisely where you are most vulnerable to offense. Insecurity is the mechanism of offense. The potential for offense always forms at that place of our deepest need. And when we find ourselves offended, our insecurity will either be exposed or aggravated.

* * *

In high school, one of my classmates had a reputation for skill-fully insulting other kids. The guys would egg him on, directing his attention to some rival or any awkward kid who unfortunately happened to be nearby, and he would cut loose with a line of insults that could peel flesh off even the most guarded. They credited his power of insult to his clever and malicious vocabulary, but, looking back, I think his real insight was his ability to see insecurity.

Most of us were too worried about covering our own insecurities to recognize each other's. While we often traded verbal jabs as a way of camaraderie, none of us intentionally aimed at each other's weak spots. What made his insults so potent was his ability to strike at a person's deepest, most vulnerable sense of themselves. He could see a person's insecurity as if they were wearing it on a T-shirt. He saw it even when his target failed to know it was there. Those insecurities made them susceptible in ways he knew how to exploit. As teenage boys, we also weren't mature enough to recognize his cruelty was a way of avoiding his own insecurities.

No one wants to admit they are insecure. We sure don't want others to see it. So, we learn early in life to ignore it, suppress it, and at all costs deny it. We learn to compensate for our insecurity through cruelty, or the pursuit of wealth, romance, titles, or the perfect physique. It's a trick we play. Carve out some modest measure of control, any control, in one area, and it might be enough to quiet the insecurity of another. What we want to avoid is being honest about how insecurity motivates us. Being honest about insecurity can unnerve even the most stoic. We all sense that insecurity is vulnerability. And no one wants to be vulnerable.

The truth is, to be human, at least an honest one, is to be insecure. We are vulnerable. We live each day in these bodies of flesh, ready to be pierced, popped, and drained of life from an endless line of threats. We are left to worry about everything from the microscopically invisible flesh-eating amoeba to the catastrophic planet-killing asteroid. For all of humanity's advancements, we still worry about weather, disease, war, and hunger. Not to mention the insecurities of a receding hairline, expanding waistline, and ballooning credit card debt. Of course, we're insecure. Humanity is plagued by vulnerability.

What can you do but hope to distract yourself from thinking about it? Go ahead, stick out your chest, raise your chin, and refuse to give it any attention. But doesn't that kind of feigned pride only give away your insecurity more? Isn't that just a cheap trick to look like you have control? Writer Allan Watts explained, "The desire for security and the feeling of insecurity are the same thing. To hold your breath is to lose your breath. A society based on the quest for security is nothing but a breath-retention contest in which everyone is as taut as a drum and as purple as a beet."[5] Most of us live holding our breath, hoping we can ignore the insecurity or numb it.

It's hard to admit our vulnerability. The rich young man's wealth, youth, influence, and especially religiosity have long disguised our insecurities. They're our best means of holding our breath and hoping not to be found out. These excuses convince most, and most of the time, convince us. But it only works because we all have things to hide. It works because we're all playing the same game. We all know the emperor's naked, but our insecurity keeps us playing along. Plus, insecurity continues to convince the king that no one can tell. No one dares say what is obvious to all. We're all too scared to admit it, too desperate in our pretending to say it. We control nothing.

To the rich young man's credit, he came with a question that acknowledged his need. He recognized his accumulation wasn't working. Something was still missing. He recognized some amount of his own insecurity. But he seemed to think of it as a remaining margin to be completed. He came to Jesus looking for advice, technique, insider information, one more thing he could acquire or achieve. He wasn't prepared to see how great his need actually was.

Continuing the conversation, the man asked Jesus, "What must I do?" Jesus answered, "Keep the commandments." That's the kind of answer that annoys us, so obvious it's almost insulting. If your teenager complained they needed money, you might suggest they "get a job." When they're tired, you say, "Go to bed." Hungry? "You should have finished your plate at dinner." Your kids will roll their eyes. It's not the answer they were looking for. You've told them what they already knew. That is the kind of answer Jesus gave the young man. Keep the commandments? Well, every Jew knew that answer. And as the young man quickly pointed out, "I've kept the commandments since childhood."[6] He hadn't risked being vulnerable for that answer.

There may be no such thing as a stupid question, but there are questions that reveal ulterior motives. Our questions often give away things we hadn't intended. The young man's question, while on the topic of religion, showed very little interest in God. He viewed God's law as something to manage, track, and collect, as if the security of the eternal life he sought was some rare collector item that, once found, could solve all his problems. He really thought security and eternal life were something he could acquire.

OUR IMPULSE TO COLLECT

My urge to collect started as a child with Star Wars action figures. They were five dollars at Walmart, and I evaluated the cost of everything else by that currency for many years. Twenty dollars was four Star Wars action figures. Still, the eighty-dollar Millennium Falcon might as well have been a million dollars. Eventually, I turned my attention to baseball cards, then coins, and, for a short time, Pogs. Unfortunately, nothing I collected is valuable today.

According to the *Wall Street Journal*, Americans spend about $1.2 trillion a year on nonessential goods, with the average American household owning 300,000 items. [7] And according to the Department of Energy, one out of four homes with a two-car garage cannot park a car inside either bay due to all the clutter. Despite occasional social movements toward minimalism and scaling down, we produce more stuff, buy more stuff, and go deeper into debt to get it every year. Before you panic thinking that I'm coming for those boxes of collectibles in your attic, my interest is in what motivates our collecting.

Psychologists have offered a wide range of explanations for the human impulse to collect. Freud posited that the traumatic experience of potty training, in which a child's possessions, i.e., their waste, was flushed away, created a sense of loss and an impulse to hoard.[8] Other scientists have linked collecting to a loss of past love and a need to surround ourselves with familiar objects for comfort. Some evolutionary biologists see collecting as a demonstration of wealth that could help entice a potential mate. I'll leave you to psychoanalyze your own collecting habits, but one fact seems true across the theories: our possessions give us a sense of security and control. We collect because it feels good to possess. Adding things feels like progress, which feels like achievement, which by comparison feels like competency. We know our collection of potted plants can't save us, but they can distract us from what we can't control. Collecting gives us an illusion of progress.

It's not just physical things. We collect emotionally, relationally, and spiritually. The rich young man who came to Jesus had collected plenty of physical possessions, but he collected more than wealth. His wealth helped him pursue religious achievements. He carefully collected a reputation of the right actions, words, and worship. He sought a life of accumulation: objects, wealth, titles, influence, competence, and religious acts.

For some people, the impulse to collect becomes obsessive and overpowering, but most of us are happy with a more modest collection of a good reputation. You need not have every toy or new release. You just need more than your friend or neighbor. We prefer to be just slightly ahead. We need just enough to impress.

We need only to be better than most of the people we know. That's just enough to quit the insecurity. Just enough to feel generally in control. We know we need to do good and are happy to do it. But what interests us is how much good really counts. Which laws? What is really required of me? How much is enough?

C. S. Lewis recognized this impulse. He wrote,

> Pride gets no pleasure out of having something, only out of having more of it than the next man. We say that people are proud of being rich, or clever, or good-looking, but they are not. They are proud of being richer, or cleverer, or better-looking than others. If everyone else became equally rich, or clever, or good-looking there would be nothing to be proud about. It is the comparison that makes you proud: the pleasure of being above the rest."[9]

Comparison works well to quiet insecurity. But it cannot cure us of it.

Perhaps Jesus sensed that the man's platitudes—calling Jesus "good teacher"—were not real respect. Might it have been nothing more than self-measured comparison? The young man's flattery may simply have been part of how he measured the world and sought to control it. Jesus was good because, by comparison, he seemed to possess something the young man lacked. The young man saw people in relationship to what they could provide to him. He measured others by his own insecurity. He came to Jesus not for Jesus's sake but for his own. He came to acquire what, by his comparisons, he still lacked, and Jesus, by his confidence, seemed to possess.

While Freud may have had unique views on why we collect physical objects, he did understand how often humans use religion to acquire things for themselves. Freud wrote, "Religion is an attempt to get control over the sensory world, in which we are placed, by means of the wish-world. . . . Its doctrines carry with them the stamp of the times in which they originated, the ignorant childhood days of the human race."[10] I think Freud got it entirely right and completely wrong.

Some acts of morality are done only to keep control: righteousness that is done only as self-righteousness; worship that attempts to acquire things for our own sake. That's always been the case. But that impulse is not due to childishness nor is that the heart of true religion. That scheme and the motivation to collect morality is the impulse of insecure adults, wise to the vulnerabilities of their own lives and desperate to find any means of controlling it. Infants are born into the same need, but the impulse to solve it for ourselves is a sign of our coming of age. We do not grow out of wishful thinking and desperate hoarding.

Our own coming of age—individually and culturally—seems only to have aggravated our feeling of insecurity. We live in an era in which our impulse to collect and consume has no limits. As institutions continue to collapse, religion dwindles, and our collective identities are replaced with the pressing need for individuality, we feel increasingly less security or control. There are now fewer places to turn for help. We have always been insecure, but we now have fewer sources for mitigating it. Watts observes:

> There is, then, the feeling that we live in a time of unusual insecurity. In the past hundred years so many long-established traditions have broken down—traditions of family and social life, of government, of the economic order, and of religious belief. As the years go by, there seem to be fewer and fewer rocks to which we can hold,

fewer things which we can regard as absolutely right and true, and fixed for all time.

To some this is a welcome release from the restraints of moral, social, and spiritual dogma. To others it is a dangerous and terrifying breach with reason and sanity, tending to plunge human life into hopeless chaos. To most, perhaps, the immediate sense of release has given a brief exhilaration, to be followed by the deepest anxiety. For if all is relative, if life is a torrent without form or goal in whose flood absolutely nothing save change itself can last, it seems to be something in which there is "no future" and thus no hope.[11]

Jesus led the rich young ruler into a moment of honesty. Frustrated by the answer he was getting, he finally exposed himself in his question. Which laws was the question at the bottom of his interest in Jesus. In Greek, it was just one word, but don't let the question's simplicity deceive you. Everything hung on that question. Bonhoeffer wrote, "The very devil lurks beneath this question."[12] "Jesus sees through his question and knows it to be the question of a piety shaped and centered in the self."[13] This was not the first time a question like that had exposed human insecurity.

THAT QUESTION FROM THE GARDEN

In the beginning, God made all things, including man and woman. He looked down on his new creation and called it good. There was a garden with rivers running through it, fruit trees, and grazing animals. All humanity needed was abundant and spread out before them. Man was created from the ground and woman from his side.

There was union between them and also with God. Bone of bone and flesh of flesh. God with them in the cool of the morning. And all of God's creative work concluded with the symbolically loaded description, "The man and his wife were both naked and were not ashamed."[14]

You could simplify it by saying they felt secure, but that wouldn't be nearly as poetic. We are not talking about securing bank accounts or home security systems, but security is precisely what they experienced. They were naked and unashamed. They felt no compulsion to cover themselves, neither from the elements of nature nor from one another's gaze. Nothing was missing. Nothing was left out. Their sense of security was both physiological and psychological. No shame, no humiliation, no embarrassment. No sense of vulnerability. No insecurity, at least none they could conceive of. Life was very good.

But in the garden was also a serpent. Scripture says he was cunning and crafty, wise enough to avoid telling the first couple what they ought to do. Instead, he asked a simple question that broke Eden. The serpent asked Eve, "Did God actually say, 'You shall not eat of any tree in the garden?'"[15] That question can be understood in a couple of ways. You could read it as a question of clarification. The serpent simply asked what God had forbidden. Or the question could be rhetorical hyperbole, not really a question at all. It's asked with no expectation of an answer but rather to make a point. What kind of God would command you not to eat? What is he concealing? Why would he keep things from you? "Did God *really* say?"

The serpent's slippery words were the first suggestion that things might not be what they appeared. Eve, in her unsuspecting nakedness, had never considered that idea. With the serpent's question, a new possibility slipped into the heart of humanity. Might God be keeping them from something? Could they be missing out on more?

Artists and writers have long depicted the fall of man with the image of Eve holding the half-eaten forbidden fruit. But before Adam or Eve could even consider that act of disobedience, a subtler suggestion was sowed. The serpent knew that before they would rebel against God, sacrificing all he had freely given them, they would need a new desire motivated by a new insecurity. They needed to feel vulnerable. The fruit could only take on its seductive power once they feared they were missing something and were made less without it. Only then could the apple become an idol, a promise of more.

Shrewdly, the serpent whispered in Eve's ear: "Perhaps there is more." The serpent awoke insecurity. "You are missing something. What will you do about that?" By drawing Eve's attention to what had been denied, the serpent suggested something was missing. All sin forms in that insecurity. We do not trust God. We fear something is lacking. There might be more. We cannot really trust God for it. We must find it on our own. There is something we must have.

In his commentary on Genesis, physician Leon Kass explains,

As long as any need is easily and simply satisfied, it goes virtually unrecognized; in the absence of obstacles, food is taken for granted, and eating proceeds mindlessly. By raising the prospect of opposition to human eating, the serpent's question brings felt need into consciousness, against the imagined possibility of its denial. And by blaming (albeit falsely) this denial on a nay-saying God, it stirs a sense of precarious selfhood pitted against an inhospitable world and threatened by outside imperatives. The woman is forced to discover that she has needs independent both of God's power to command them and of the world's ability to satisfy them; pondering the question, she begins to feel both her vulnerability and her independence.[16]

That combination is toxic: insecurity and our desperate need to resolve it. Eve had not yet disobeyed God, but the justification for her rebellion was laid. She was now suspicious of God. She was increasingly thinking of herself. The temptation felt empowering, but that was only a thin sugar coating to mask the taste of the real pill, the insecurity she had already swallowed whole. Having begun with food, the serpent pressed the insecurity deeper. If God withheld good food, what else was he withholding?

Eve corrected the serpent, pointing out that God had only forbidden them from eating from a single tree at the center of the garden, but even her correction seemed to further fixate her attention on what had been forbidden. Her vision shifted from all the goodness of teeming creation to a single tree, a single fruit, a single desire. Having drawn her attention to that lone object of prohibition, the serpent used God's command to aggravate Eve's new sense of insecurity. "You will not surely die," the serpent said. "For God knows that when you eat of it your eyes will be opened, and you will be like God, knowing good and evil."[17]

Of course, what the serpent implied was that Eve's eyes were currently closed. So, Eve's sense of need shifted from food to knowledge and the possibility that she could obtain what God had. Her vision left the fruit and turned inward on herself. "When the woman saw that the tree was good for food, and that it was a delight to the eyes, and that the tree was to be desired to make one wise, she took of its fruit and ate."[18]

The fruit did not have secret power. It was not laced with the poison of evil. As is still true today, the object—the idol—never really matters. It is what we make of the idol, what we need it to be, that corrupts. The seductive nature of an idol lies in taking it for ourselves, in attempting to acquire our own solution to our own need. By the satanic lie, Eve had conferred on that fruit the hopes of her rebellion and the desperate fear of her new insecurity. The serpent could have sold her any snake oil, and Eve would have gladly traded all she possessed to obtain it. We will sacrifice everything to cure our insecurity. The fruit was simply the object that promised the cure. And it did open her eyes, but not in the way she imagined.

Having eaten the fruit, Adam and Eve immediately realized their nakedness. That revelation came with a new impulse to cover themselves. The fruit did not alleviate their insecurity; it exacerbated it. They saw what they hadn't before: they were desperately vulnerable on their own. They panicked when they saw it. They sewed fig leaves and hid in bushes. The nakedness that had previously demonstrated their security in God's creation now revealed their new sense of insecurity. Imagine how that first realization of vulnerability must have felt.

Before being banished from the garden, as if to remind them of their inadequacy for the task they now faced, God replaced their makeshift fig leaf clothes with ones made of animal skin. From that moment, the world would be one of conflict, suffering, pain, toil, blame, and the constant effort to hold together what Adam and Eve had broken. Death entered the scene. Expelled from the garden, humanity could no longer survive naked. Creation was no longer a paradise. Humankind became weighed down with the full knowledge of good and evil. We tasted insecurity and now carry it in our broken bodies.

INSECURITY AND OFFENSE

In 2018, researchers Isabella Poggi and Francesca D'Errico studied the psychological experience of offense. Though we usually associate offense with public insult or rudeness, Poggi and D'Errico suspected that offense has its roots, not in external actions alone, but in each person's inner insecurity. They poured through thousands of personal essays and survey questions, searching for patterns in how participants described the experience of being offended. Their work was published in the *Frontiers of Psychology* in which they concluded that the feeling of offense was not about threats to a person's external reputation but instead their internal self-image. They concluded:

> An offense is a wound, an injury to the soul, an attack to something even more important than the integrity of our body: our image. We feel offended every time we think that someone conceives—and possibly communicates to ourselves or others—an evaluation of us that is worse/lower than one we think we deserve. Yet, this wound is particularly serious since it does not only sully the image that the offender or others have of us, but nicks an even more precious good of ours: our self-image.[19]

Picking up the language from their participants' surveys, Poggi and D'Errico wrote,

> All negative emotions have the function to alert the subject that an important goal is at risk of being thwarted, and to

induce immediate reactions aimed at a repair. Here, the very pain of feeling offended alerts us that our goals of image and self-image are challenged.[20]

According to the research, offense alerts you that something deeply personal is at stake and being challenged. You have been actively building a self-image, a sense of who you are, and when that self-image is denied recognition or criticized by another, it hurts. The worst forms of offense seem to be connected to our insecurities. There is a direct relationship between insecurity and offense.

If a stranger approached you on the street and called you dumb, it's not hard to recover. You would probably conclude they must be insane. You would find little threat from their words. Few would even take them seriously. You might call it insulting, but most wouldn't call it an offense. It's too random and wild to be offensive. But if a close friend jokes at a dinner party about your lower IQ and you really do feel insecure about your intellect, it hits differently. You're much more likely to call their insensitivity offensive.

What makes one comment rude and the other offensive is your preexisting insecurities. The experience of offense has as much to do with the sensitivity of your insecurities as it does with the severity of the offending action or words. A person with no insecurities would theoretically never experience offense, while a person deeply insecure will continually find cause for offense, even in the slightest acts of omission. Though you may not use the language to describe it, I'm guessing you've seen and felt it in yourself, too. Insecurity is the trigger that begins the mechanism of offense. It's the boot at the beginning of Mouse Trap. When you feel offended, it's your own insecurities that should draw your attention.

WHAT TO DO WITH INSECURITY

How did Jesus ultimately answer the young man's questions? He did not whisper a secret. He did not offer some advanced tactic or a magic word. Instead, Jesus again offered the most basic answer. "Which laws?" Jesus simply quoted from the Ten Commandments. "You shall not murder, You shall not commit adultery, You shall not steal, You shall not bear false witness, Honor your father and mother, and, You shall love your neighbor as yourself."[21] You can hear the young man in his mind checking off each item on Jesus's list. As quickly as Jesus finished, the man blurted out, "All these I have kept."[22] He was so quick to justify himself that he missed what Jesus had done.

Jesus had only quoted part of the Ten Commandments. He had only quoted the observable second half of the rules. These were what the man was interested in, what could be seen. I'm sure the man had refrained from murder, and adultery, and theft. But the absence of the first commandments should have drawn the young man's attention. What about the Sabbath? What about the Lord's name? What about the command to have no other gods?

Claiming to have fulfilled the observable law without any reference to the first of the commandments misunderstood the law and its real test entirely. For this young man, the law was like all his other achievements. They were not only doable but were a sign of his success: wealth, position, respect, righteousness. If the man had understood Jesus's teaching, if he had perceived the law's real purpose, his questions would have been very different. His question should have been, "How?" How can the law be fulfilled? How can my life ever be good enough? How, given our inability to secure our own lives, can any of us have eternal life? How can anyone find eternal security? But the rich young man could not identify himself with that kind of need. He had spent his life doing exactly the opposite.

After the man left, Jesus's disciples came to him with their own question. They were amazed by what Jesus had said and how the conversation had deteriorated. They asked Jesus, "Who then can be saved?" If a man of such wealth and influence could not follow, who could? Jesus answered them, "With man this is impossible, but with God all things are possible."[23] Salvation is impossible for us. Self-made security is impossible. Our only hope is to come to him in a posture of need.

Recall the Beatitudes: "Blessed are those who are poor in spirit. . . . Blessed are those who mourn. . . . Blessed are the meek . . . [and] those who hunger and thirst for righteousness. . . . Blessed are those who are persecuted."[24] But those are the very things religion is supposed to help us avoid. We keep the law, give, and obey so that we won't be poor or hungry or defeated. No other religion calls these things blessed. Religion exists to help you escape vulnerability, and yet Jesus suggested that we must humble ourselves and become like a child.[25] We must become vulnerable. We must abandon our work to secure life for ourselves. We must embrace our insecurity as the place God wants to begin. Jesus said the opposite of what everyone believed. We come to God through our need, not our righteousness.

"Go and sell all your possessions. Empty yourself of your collection. And follow me."[26] That was Jesus's advice for the young man. Embrace your insecurity. Put yourself in a physical state that will remind you of your spiritual one. Abandon your attempts at control and follow. What Jesus asked the man to own was his vulnerability. Jesus does not seek, like the world, to distract us from it or to cover it up. Jesus teaches us to embrace our state of insecurity.

The young man's problem was not, in the end, about selling things or becoming poor. It was about his trust and dependence on what he had collected for his security. Embracing his insecurity was exactly what the man couldn't do. It is what so few are willing to do. By refusing to come to God and embracing our insecurity, we only aggravate it and doom ourselves to an insecurity far worse. It's not hard to see how the insecurity intensifies.

INVENTING OUR OWN SOLUTION

The German philosopher Friedrich Nietzsche well predicted our present situation when he published *The Parable of The Madman* in 1882. He wrote of a man who moved throughout his town declaring the death of God. But God had not died of age or sickness. Humanity had killed him. In church services and in the streets, the man interrupted, "We have killed him—you and I. All of us are his murderers. But how did we do this? How could we drink up the sea? Who gave us the sponge to wipe away the entire horizon? What were we doing when we unchained this earth from its sun?"[27]

The man, whom the crowds thought to be mad, was trying to help them see the consequences of what they had done. It took a supposed madman to see it. But he proved not to be mad at all. He was prophetic. Nietzsche recognized that too often true words are quickly and easily dismissed. They were content in their new disbelief, even empowered by it, but Nietzsche realized that though they had disposed of God, the human heart still worshipped. They had not solved their deepest needs. And far from abandoning religion, humanity would have to reinvent religion for this new age. Humanity would have to find an answer to insecurity, and it would have to do it without reference to God.

The madman explained,

What was holiest and mightiest of all that the world has yet owned has bled to death under our knives: who will wipe this blood off us? What water is there for us to clean ourselves? What festivals of atonement, what sacred games shall we have to invent? Is not the greatness of this deed too great for us? Must we ourselves not become gods simply to appear worthy of it?[28]

Nietzsche did not see the death of God as a cause to celebrate but recognized that such a supposed loss would require a new kind of religion.

Humanity, having never known a world without the divine, couldn't simply walk away from what had previously given meaning to all of existence. We would have to find new means of atonement. We would have to invent new sacred games. We would have to find some new source of security. Nietzsche recognized that the only place humanity had left to turn was itself. We must become our own gods. He identified the new position of insecurity in which we have placed ourselves.

Nietzsche asked, "Are we not plunging continually? Backward, sideward, forward, in all directions? Is there still any up or down? Are we not straying, as through an infinite nothing? Do we not feel the breath of empty space? Has it not become colder? Is not night continually closing in on us? Do we not need to light lanterns in the morning?"[29] The madman was describing a new and deeper insecurity. Gone were any fixed horizons of morality, and the consequences were disorientation and uncertainty.

The crowd stared at the madman in confusion. "I have come too early," he confessed, smashing his lantern on the ground. "Deeds, though done, still require time to be seen and heard."[30] It would take time for humanity to fully understand what it had done. It would take time for us to understand we were once again naked and to go about reconstructing our fig-leaf clothes.

Commenting on Nietzsche's parable of the madman, René Girard wrote,

> It is a richer reading than the "death of God." The text is speaking about the birth of religion as well as its death, because they amount to the same thing. The most revealing sentence is the one that says that God's death forces the murderers to invent a new religious cult.[31]

The real question that emerged from Nietzsche's parable is, what kind of new religion would we create? What would replace God? What would we do with our insecurities if we could no longer entrust them to God?

Nietzsche saw the coming of a new kind of religion in which we would look within for the divine, in which our idols would become images of ourselves. It would not be a world without worship. There is no escaping the impulse to worship. Something still catches our eye. Something still holds our attention. Some image still forms in our insecurity. As postmodern writer David Foster Wallace admitted,

> Because here's something else that's weird but true: in the day-to-day trenches of adult life, there is actually no such thing as atheism. There is no such thing as not worshipping. Everybody worships. The only choice we get is what to worship.[32]

The only question left is where we turn for security. Can we even find what we're looking for?

Insecurity inevitably leads to the desire for some salvific object. Insecurity always leads us to worship. It awakens our imagination and sends our eyes looking for an image of security. Insecurity leads you to an idol. Recognize your insecurity and you'll always find some fruit promising to solve it.

* * *

"Truly, I say to you, whoever does not receive the kingdom of God like a child shall not enter it." — Mark 10:15

CHAPTER 4

OBSESSION: "YOU HYPOCRITES!"

"Then the disciples came and said to him, 'Do you know that the Pharisees were offended when they heard this saying?' He answered, 'Every plant that my heavenly Father has not planted will be rooted up. Let them alone; they are blind guides.'"

MATTHEW 15:12-14

"A man sits in front of a bad television program and doesn't know that he is bored. . . . Theologians and philosophers have been saying for a century that God is dead, but what we confront now is the possibility that 'man is dead,' transformed into a thing, a producer, a consumer, an idolater of other things."

ERICH FROMM

Jesus was teaching in the region of Gennesaret, a small sloping plane on the western shore of the Sea of Galilee. The crowds were growing as talk of his miracles and healings spread. Word of Jesus's ministry had gone far beyond those scattered Jewish towns of the Galilee. Leaders in Jerusalem had heard, and a commission of Pharisees and legal scribes were sent to investigate. While the crowds spoke of his power, the religious leaders were concerned about a rumor of Jesus having violated traditional practices.

The religious leaders were concerned that Jesus's disciples were not keeping up the traditions of cleanliness and purity. Observing Jesus, they noticed that his disciples did not properly wash their hands before meals. That seems small, but it was coloring Jesus's ministry with a growing reputation of impropriety. Jesus associated with unclean people, failed to keep certain oral traditions, and was spreading his teaching to a growing crowd of followers. The Pharisees wasted no time vocalizing their concerns.

Though often at odds, Jesus was more like the Pharisees than any other group in first-century Judea. His willingness to engage the Pharisees throughout the Gospels demonstrates their common concerns for righteousness and obedience to the law. The Pharisees were motivated by a deep conviction that God's law should be obeyed in every aspect of life. They sought to push back against the cultural influence of Romanization. We misread the Gospels and miss the important point Jesus sought to make by too quickly writing the Pharisees off as Jesus's opponents. Jesus spoke some of his harshest words to the Pharisees, not out of spite or disdain, but because he recognized what, in their zeal, had blinded them. The Pharisees were falling into the same mechanism of offense that plagues every human. They tried to solve their insecurity with their own traditions, regulations, and effort. Their growing obsession with their tradition was leading them into the trap.

Insecurity was settled deep in the Jewish identity. From their exiled homes of Babylon, the Jews recognized the mistakes they and their fathers had made. They had experienced God's judgment because of their disobedience. They determined they needed a renewed focus on the law. Obedience was their solution. The Mishnah, written about 200 CE, collected into writing the much older oral traditions that had been growing since the time of the Jewish exile to Babylon (597–538 BCE). You can observe in the Mishnah the growing obsession of meticulous obedience driven by that fear. The Mishnah recommended that teachers "make a fence around the Torah." The idea was that if a tradition of rules and regulations could be formed around the sacred laws of the Torah, they could protect the Jews from coming too near disobedience and so secure the full blessings of God. Obedience was a strategy.

Hundreds of regulations and oral traditions began to build up around the law. The complex system of rules the Pharisees sought to enforce was not random. They were a means of protecting obedience to God. They were designed to keep Israel holy and were motivated by a determination to never again be exiled or judged as their fathers had been before them. Their oral tradition was their answer to the question of their insecurity and the ongoing threat of their own potential unfaithfulness. They feared the loss of God's blessing, so they sought to protect and regulate it through obedience.

When the Pharisees saw Jesus's disciples eating with unwashed hands—which was not prohibited in the written law but was traditionally prohibited by their oral customs—they felt unnerved. Too much depended on the system they had built. They asked Jesus, "Why do your disciples break the tradition of the elders?"[1] Jesus did not take the debate but turned the question. He suggested that the Pharisees did far worse. Jesus explained how they instead routinely broke the commandments of God to protect their tradition. "You hypocrites," he charged them. "Well did Isaiah prophesy of you, when he said: 'This people honors me with their lips, but their heart is far from me; in vain do they worship me, teaching as doctrines the commandments of men.'"[2]

Those were strong words. And Jesus poked at the deepest and most sensitive part of their insecurity. All their carefully observed regulations were not real worship. Their own prophet Isaiah had prophesied against them. Jesus quoted the same passage of Isaiah that predicted the destruction of Jerusalem that led to the very exile the Pharisees were trying so desperately to correct. It was the Pharisees who risked exile, not Jesus. Isaiah also prophesied that God would someday do a new work amongst his people, writing, "I will again do wonderful things with this people, with wonder upon wonder."[3] In that one quotation, Jesus pinpointed the Pharisees' insecurity and suggested that they were missing what God was now doing by their obsession with their own system of control.

The Pharisees withdrew, now more opposed to Jesus and his teaching. It was not over. The tension between them would continue to build. Jesus's disciples quickly raised their own concerns. "Do you know that the Pharisees were offended when they heard this saying?"[4] they asked Jesus.

Who wouldn't be offended by being called a hypocrite? When we hear the word *hypocrisy*, we imagine a person who says one thing and does another. How could Jesus charge the Pharisees with that? Their issue was not failing to follow through with their own commands. No one took consistency more seriously than the Pharisees. The hypocrisy Jesus recognized was that disparity had formed in the focus of their attention. They had traded God for tradition, worship for discipline, and true teaching for human commands. Like Peter, whose eyes had shifted from Jesus to the world, the Pharisees in their insecurity had shifted their gaze from God to themselves. They had turned their tradition into an idol.

Their worship had turned into an obsession with themselves, their insecurity driving it.

Jesus did for the Pharisees exactly what he had done for Peter. The Pharisees had come to rebuke him, and Jesus turned it back on them. Jesus attempted to shock them into seeing their blindness and the false worship at work in their own hearts. The words of Isaiah became an obstacle in their pursuit, and they stumbled on it. They left offended.

* * *

Obsession is always a good warning sign of idolatry. But to suggest to the Pharisees that they were worshiping idols would have mortified them. During the time of Jesus, the Jews believed they had mostly cleaned up Israel's idolatry problem. The Talmud, in another collection of the rabbinic traditions, concluded that the temptation of idolatry had been slaughtered. Some even boasted that the leaders of the great Rabbinical Assembly had shut up idolatry in a barrel.[5] It was true that in Jesus's day, a physical idol was hard to find in a Jewish town or home. Archaeologists still recognize Jewish settlements from the period by the absence of images. The Jews forbid not only idols but any image of a living thing, human or animal.

If you define an idol as an actual physical object, they were surely the least idolatrous generation since the beginning of time. But as the prophets had already warned them, idols are not always carved statues. Images are not always physical. An image can be imagined. An idol can form in the heart. What the Pharisees had done was carve an image out of their own self-righteous effort.

The New Testament Scholar G. K. Beale writes, "In Jesus' time [idolatry] manifested itself not by worshipping stone or wooden idols but human-made tradition."[6] The religious teachers and scribes of Jesus's day might not have carved images, but they walked around with distinct images in their minds. They had an image of an ideal obedient Jew, which all but guaranteed divine blessing. Those images became their source of security. Everything depended on living up to those images. They trusted their own obedience. So, gradually but undeniably, their attention shifted. They were no longer worshiping God; they were worshiping an image of themselves. It was increasingly dominating their whole perspective on life and God. Jesus recognized it.

Perhaps Jesus made the point most clearly in his parable of the Pharisee and the tax collector. Luke records Jesus's description of two men who went up to the temple to pray. One was a Pharisee and the other a tax collector.[7] Lifting his eyes to heaven, the Pharisee thanked the Lord that he was not like other men: unjust, extortioners, and adulterers. Instead, he fasted twice a week and paid his tithe.

What was this man doing if not chiseling an image? He carved it not with his hands but with his imagination. He formed an ideal of himself, and he held that self-image as the source of his identity, blessing, and security. Did he not carry a graven image of security with him?

Some distance away, the tax collector also prayed, but he could not bring himself to look to heaven. He only beat his chest and prayed, "God, be merciful to me, a sinner!"[8] Concluding the parable, Jesus suggested that the tax collector went home justified while the Pharisee did not. The tax collector needed God; the Pharisee needed only himself.

What really differentiated those two men? Their recognition of need. The tax collector understood it and embraced it. He was hopeless and desperately in need of God's salvation. His insecurity was evident to him and probably others as well. The Pharisee could not see his condition. He imagined himself secure because of the careful image of piety he had diligently worked to construct. He could not let go of it.

It was functionally the same practice of idolatry that continues to plague the human heart, but perhaps those carved statues are easier to recognize than the idols we imagine. For that reason, Jesus reserved some of his strongest words of offense for the Pharisees. He challenged them, "For you are like whitewashed tombs, which outwardly appear beautiful, but within are full of dead people's bones and all uncleanness. So you also outwardly appear righteous to others, but within you are full of hypocrisy and lawlessness."[9] What Jesus sought to confront was the idol they made of themselves.

Who among us keeps carved figures in a hidden niche? Who today fashions gods out of stone or wood? We do not imagine ourselves idolaters. But we are as blind to it as the Pharisees. Where there is insecurity, there will soon be an image, an idol that promises to solve it. That is how idolatry has always worked. Insecurity drives the imagination to find an image, an ideal to rescue us. Idols are promises of security. We create idols first by imagining them. That is not ancient pagan religion; that is the way of every human heart. Insecurity leads to an obsession with some object of desire. It does so through the darkened imagination, which promises us salvation.

IDOLATRY FORMS IN INSECURITY

Beale defines an idol as "whatever your heart clings to or relies on for ultimate security."[10] We worship to try and find security. We search for a solution, a salvation, a means of control. Eve's imagination worked that fruit into an idol that promised to deliver what God had withheld. The fruit became something more as Eve saw that it was good not just to eat but also to make one wise. But Adam and Eve soon discovered that while idols form in relation to our insecurity, they do not rescue us from it; they make it worse. Biblical scholar Richard Lints explains:

> An idol is desired as a means to an end, and the end is significance and security on the individual's own terms. Since significance and security cannot be fulfilled by the idol, the idol creates a deeper longing for significance and security for that which it cannot provide. This results in a chasing after the idol, driven by the conviction that eventually the idol will somehow provide the promised significance and security.[11]

Lints describes how our minds fixate and obsess over solutions we've imagined. You can see it in the obsessive qualities of the Pharisees, but you've no doubt experienced it in your own life. Perhaps you grew up in poverty and have spent many hours daydreaming of wealth and success. Maybe those middle school taunts left you self-conscious, and now you can't help but fixate on every extra pound and blemish. It could be a past pain that's left you constantly anxious and determined to trust no one again. The reasons are endless but the result is the same. You become desperate and absorbed. An idol begins to possess you as it is constantly more present in your thinking. What you obsess over is a version of yourself secure from vulnerability. The insecurity projects a solution that you carry as an image in your heart. You have your idol, and yet still, the insecurity only grows worse and the obsession more controlling.

Writing in the book *Identity and Idolatry*, Lints observes,

The gods created in the deep recesses of the human longing for security were dangerous in a surprising fashion. Though they did not 'exist' in an ontological sense, they exercised enormous sway over those who had made them. They took on a virtual life of their own."[12]

It's no wonder the ancients imagined their idols to be alive.

Seeing such obsession in the ancient worship of physical idols can help you recognize it in your own heart. The world is dangerous and unpredictable. To survive, the ancients needed sun and rain, peace from their enemies, and children to aid in work and continue civilization. But like the first couple's attempt to cover themselves with fig leaves, humanity soon learned the precarious nature of weather, war, and fertility. There are things we can't secure. For all our technological advancements, we still know the pain associated with each. We still starve, still die by the sword, are still swept away by wind and waves, and we still grieve the loss of life. For the ancients, trusting in an unseen god felt too disempowering. They needed forces, powers, and gods they could control. They needed something they could see. So, as the apostle Paul explained, "Claiming to be wise, they became fools, and exchanged the glory of the immortal God for images resembling mortal man and birds and animals and creeping things."[13]

Do not imagine the ancients to be naively superstitious. Don't roll your eyes at their primitive worship of some animal image. The idols they carved were symbols, mechanisms by which they sought to harness the powers beyond normal human control. They were perhaps even more aware of their own limitations than we are. And as we will see, their attempts to find any means of security were not so different from our own.

The Old Testament book of Exodus offers the predominant example of idolatry. Having been freed from Egyptian slavery and miraculously delivered from the Egyptian military, the Hebrew people found themselves at the base of Mount Sinai, where Moses had been gone far longer than expected. He was definitely their leader whom they had seen stand before Pharaoh, who had led them out of the city, and by whose staff the waters had parted for their rescue. They could see and follow him. But his prolonged absence unnerved them. They did not know where they were going. They were unaccustomed to the wilderness around them. And now they feared they were without their leader. They needed something they could see. An invisible deity and an absent Moses worsened their insecurity. So, the people pressed Aaron to make them an idol.[14]

The Hebrews had seen plenty of idols during their stay in Egypt. Egyptian religion was awash in images of the gods. *The World History Encyclopedia* catalogs over two thousand Egyptian deities.[15] They had gods for every need and natural force. Gods related to the sun and moon, stars, weather, rivers, and just about every animal: cats, cows, and crocodiles. The Egyptians were obsessed with images. They carved images of their gods and built visual monuments to display their power: pyramids, sphinxes, thrones, and stone reliefs of great conquests and religious festivals. Their sorcerers and priests cataloged and studied signs and omens and, for a while, even emulated the opening judgments recorded in the Exodus.

What did the fleeing Hebrews have? An old man with a staff? A pillar of fire now stalled on the mountain? They had no monuments, no pantheons, no images of their god. With Moses seemingly gone, their insecurity worsened, and they reverted to what they knew. They needed something they could see. They needed an image to help them feel secure. They needed an object by which God could be followed and upon which they could place their trust. So they took off their gold, and Aaron cast them a figure of a calf. Seeing the freshly minted golden image, the people proclaimed, "These are your gods, O Israel, who brought you up out of the land of Egypt!"[16]

Their confidence suddenly returned; they partied. They indulged themselves in drunken revelry. They had their god. They could see him and could carry him around for good luck. They needed an image of God to help soothe their insecurity, and they did what they saw everyone else doing. They imagined one and then self-constructed it at their own cost.

That act became the paradigmatic sin of Israel in the Bible. They exchanged the invisible God for an image inspired by the religion of their neighbors. They gave up the living God for one they had created. And so, over and over, Israel gave up the invisible God for ones they could see: the gods of Egypt, Philistia, Syria, and Babylon, to name a few.

The prophets were all over them for it, mocking these man-made gods. Ridiculing Israel for trusting in objects made of metal, wood, and stone. Still, the land of Israel became littered with pagan temples, altars, and idols. They couldn't seem to help themselves. With the Israelites' eyes constantly fixed on external dangers and external idols, their prophets recognized that the real idolatry was committed not with their hands, but it was playing out in their hearts.

The Old Testament prophet Ezekiel warned that the Israelites had polluted their hearts with these idols and were now stumbling over them.[17] According to Ezekiel, these hidden idols of the heart were scandalizing Israel, causing them to be offended. The idols were leading them down a path of destruction that would overwhelm them with offense. They would trip over the idols they were building. In his prophecies, Ezekiel warned them about far more than carved figures. He warned Israel that the internal mechanism by which they dealt with their insecurity had become an obsession with idols, blinding them to truth.

Ezekiel recognized that the heart, not the hand, creates idols. So, idolatry is the perennial temptation of all humanity in all times and places. You perceive images, objects, and desires that you imagine will give you security and meaning: a relationship, a physique, a home, a job, a trophy, a reputation. You imagine it and chase after it just as the ancients did their carved statues. You make them the solution to everything that unnerves you. It feels like the most natural thing. How else do you live if not in pursuit of what you want? So, as John Calvin famously put it, "Man's nature, so to speak, is a perpetual factory of idols."[18]

IDOLS FORM FIRST IN THE IMAGINATION

Tim Keller once warned, "The true god of your heart is what your thoughts effortlessly go to when there is nothing else demanding your attention."[19] I think Keller was not only right but wise to offer that tool for self-reflection. Where does your mind naturally drift? What has your attention when undistracted? What most easily turns to obsession?

Give any person a moment of free thought and usually the mind drifts to either fear or longing. Those two thoughts are not so different. In fact, they are usually the same thing. They are connected by our instinct for worship and the mechanism of idols that connect insecurity to new desires.

Idols no longer live on shelves. They live in our imagination and our obsessive imagining of what we want and who we could be. The English word *imagination* comes from the Latin imaginari, which literally means "to picture oneself." It's what our imagination does best. The French writer Joseph Joubert called the imagination the "eye of the soul."[20] Like all our faculties, the imagination is a powerful tool for good, particularly when turned outward from the self. But it has a unique tendency to self-fixate.

C. S. Lewis, beloved for his imaginative world of Narnia, also recognized the distorted tendencies of our imaginations. Lewis wrote that the imagination "has also a bad use: to provide for us, in shadowy form, a substitute for virtues, successes, distinctions *et cetera* which ought to be sought outside in the real world—e.g. picturing all I'd do if I were rich instead of earning and saving."[21] French novelist Marcel Proust also warned, "The inertia of the mind urges it to slide down the easy slope of imagination, rather than to climb the steep slope of introspection."[22] That is, our minds more naturally dream up new realities rather than wrestle with the one we're in. What we imagine seems disconnected from reality. But it's the imagination that often reveals the truth of our hearts. And yet the imagination cannot produce lasting security.

It's the oldest trick, the oldest sleight of hand. Distract the audience with some shiny object in one hand while you do the real trick with your other hand. The trick works by exploiting our eye's tendency to be easily misdirected. Our vision is lazy. It's easier to see what we assume than to see what something actually is. Promise us a solution and, once our eyes are fixed on it, you can slip even greater insecurity into our back pocket. We'll think it's been there all the time. Let me give you an example.

In one of the great works of English fiction, *Jane Eyre*, author Charlotte Brontë sought to depict the mechanism of insecurity and idolatry in just this way. Jane Eyre, the protagonist, is born into insecurity. As a child, she was orphaned and abused by the family of her vicious aunt, who punished her with isolation from others. A charity school only worsened Jane's condition, leaving her half-starved and further abandoned. The experiences took a toll on Jane's self-evaluations. She considered herself plain and unremarkable and fixated on her low social status. But Jane was also a girl with an active imagination, a tool of escape from her world of insecurity. Her imagination often helped her escape to other worlds, yet fueled by insecurity, that same imagination soon turned to obsession. As insecurity always does, it found an object upon which to place its hopes. For Jane Eyre, that idol was love.

As a child, Jane clung to a toy doll as her sole companion. She only later recognized how that object became what she could not find elsewhere. Jane explained,

> Human beings must love something, and in the dearth of worthier objects of affection, I contrived to find a pleasure in loving and cherishing a faded graven image, shabby as a miniature scarecrow. It puzzles me now to remember with what absurd sincerity I doted on this little toy; half-fancying it alive and capable of sensation, I could not sleep unless it was folded in my night-gown; and when it lay there safe and warm, I was comparatively happy, believing it to be happy likewise.[23]

As a reader, we rightfully sympathize with Jane's dependence. No child should ever be in such a position. But Jane eventually outgrew her need for the doll. Her insecurity found a new object: men. In a moment of frankness, she admitted, "If others don't love me, I would rather die than live."[24] But Jane didn't die of loneliness; she found a particular man on which to place her hopes: Edward

Rochester, an English gentleman with great wealth and an impressive estate. Jane, who was employed as the tutor and governess to Rochester's daughter, soon found herself obsessed.

Part of what makes Brontë's novel so potent—G. K. Chesterton called it the "truest book that was ever written"[25]—is Jane's self-awareness and recognition of the forces at work within her. Charlotte Brontë was a devout Christian and the daughter of a Protestant minister. Her character, Jane Eyre, was also devout in faith and seemed to recognize the religious impulses at work beneath her insecurities and obsessions. Jane described her growing infatuation with Mr. Rochester, explaining, "He stood between me and every thought of religion, as an eclipse intervenes between man and the broad sun. I could not, in those days, see God for his creature: of whom I had made an idol."[26]

That is, perhaps, the best theological definition of idolatry I have ever encountered. Brontë's analogy is a powerful one. An idol is like an eclipse. The moon is four hundred times smaller than the sun, but its proximity to our eye can still blot out its light and turn day to night. A man can replace God. Any object can—real or imagined. Our eyes fixated on it, insecurity fueling our obsession, earthly things can fill our vision and become bigger than the whole world. Insecurity makes things appear larger than they really are.

It took Jane a long time to learn the truth about Mr. Rochester. I won't spoil the ending, but all the red flags had been there. Astute readers immediately recognize that something about Mr. Rochester was wrong. Mr. Rochester was not who Jane wished him to be. Still, Jane couldn't see it. She was blind to the truth. She saw only what she wanted to see. As novelist Graham Greene writes, "Insecurity twists meanings and poisons trust."[27] Our idols always blind us; they blinded Jane, too. Idols darken the world and leave us more desperate, confused, and vulnerable in the end. They blot out the light of God's truth. As the apostle Paul put it, our minds are darkened by it.

It's not accidental that the first two commandments are positioned together. The first commandment warns of worshipping other gods, but the second commandment expands that prohibition to creating images of God. Why the ban on images? Because human nature is to worship, and human nature is to imagine the kind of god we need. Our darkened imaginations predispose us to graven images. Our imaginations have become a potent tool of idolatry.

Consider again Eve's temptation in the garden. We previously saw how the serpent drew her attention to a potential insecurity, but the serpent didn't stop there. Having awoken insecurity, the serpent directed her imagination onto an object. The serpent answered Eve, "Your eyes will be opened, and you will be like God."[28] What a thought to imagine.

Genesis next records, "So when the woman saw that the tree was good for food, and that it was a delight to the eyes, and that the tree was to be desired to make one wise, she took of its fruit and ate."[29] Insecurity and imagination infused the fruit with an alluring promise. It was no longer just a tree or a piece of fruit. She desired it for what it could give her. Idols may not be alive, but they are in our imaginations. That's enough to give them great power.

From Eve's apple to the carved gods of Egypt, Babylon, and Rome, humanity has long sought to deal with its insecurity through idolization, through worship. For what is worship but the valuing of one thing above all else? As René Girard put it, "Reality is not rational, but religious."[30] We worship idols to try and find a solution to our vulnerability.

THE IDOL OF THE SELF

As it was for the Pharisees, who could point to no physical idol, it can be difficult to recognize when our imaginations have begun the work of fashioning images of worship in our own hearts. Worse, as the insecurities of our lives shift, so do our mental infatuations and the idols formed by them. Insecurity, imagination, and the idolatry they produce are always shifting and reforming in us. Scottish theologian Thomas Chalmers described how a young man may cease to desire sensual pleasures only because his attention has shifted to material gain. We are no longer slaves to one desire because we have been taken captive by another. Chalmers writes,

> There is not one of these transformations in which the heart is left without an object. Its desire for one particular object may be conquered; but as to its desire to have some one object or another, this is unconquerable.[31]

While your imagination is constantly reshaping the idols of your heart, cultural voices and influences are also shaping those insecurities and directing those desires. As the serpent in the garden easily focused Eve's attention on the fruit, our culture also stirs up insecurities and offers potential saviors. As we saw in Nietzsche's parable of the madman, there is a modern insecurity that many living today cannot avoid. We have lost the traditional grounding of our identity and security in God. Without a God to worship, we are left with only ourselves to worship, just as Nietzsche predicted. We live in a time when the logic of meaning suggests that we must become our own gods.

As the Pharisees found themselves tempted by the imagination of their own self-righteous image, the modern imagination has become obsessed with what the Canadian philosopher Charles Taylor calls "expressive individualism,"[32] or the authentic self. We spend our days thinking about ourselves, our tastes, our interests, our unique expression of the desires of our hearts. We imagine what we want and pursue that elusive feeling of "finding ourselves." That may sound philosophically abstract, but the language the world uses to pique your imagination toward that goal should be immediately obvious. See if this sounds familiar.

Each night at the center of Disney's Magic Kingdom, a crowd of thousands gathers for a spectacular show of lights, fireworks, music, and video projection that brings the castle's turrets and walls to life with the pantheon of Disney heroes. Tourists squeeze into the central gardens with backpacks, strollers, and their souvenirs to end their magical day gazing up at the display. The technology is magic. The first time I saw it, my three-year-old son sat on my shoulders in awe. We were both in awe.

Disney's writers and directors are master storytellers, but so was the serpent. I listened as the show's narrators cut together pieces of our favorite Disney songs with a voice-over that perfectly rose and fell with the music:

> Each of us has a dream, a heart's desire. It calls to us. And when we are brave enough to listen, and bold enough to pursue it, that dream will lead us on a journey to discover who we are meant to be. All we have to do is look inside our hearts and unlock the magic within. . . . Your destiny lies within you; you just have to be brave enough to see it.[33]

Perhaps no institution has shaped our cultural imagination more over the past decades than those who "entertain" us with stories. Cultural analyst Jamie O'Boyle believes,

Disney is our national storyteller, the primary cultural 'imprinter' of what it means for children to be American. . . . Disney is so closely tied in with a national psyche of who we are, the things we like about ourselves, that we don't like the idea there's a corporation behind it. . . . As much as anything, this is about us.[34]

You can decide how much Disney is to be credited with creating culture or simply distributing it, but there's no denying Disney's impact.

With my son sitting there on my shoulders, soaking up words and images, it struck me that there was something deeply religious about what we were doing. Far from being just entertainment, the narration was talking about the great questions of life, the same questions religion has always been at the center of answering. The same questions I often take with me to the pulpit on Sunday mornings. Where do we find meaning? How can we build lives of purpose? What is most sacred and worthy of our highest attention? What is forming the images in us? How do we face the insecurities of life?

According to Disney, those questions can only be answered by each person looking within. The show's designers may have drawn our eyes upward to the spectacular views of a castle in light, but their real message was to turn our eyes inward on our own hearts. It's your heart's longings that lead to happily-ever-after. Today's heroes are those willing to risk it all in pursuit of what their heart most desires.

Charles Taylor describes this as an age of authenticity. We now seek to cure our insecurity by being brave enough to express our own unique desires. He explains that in this new secular view of meaning,

> Everyone has a right to develop their own form of life, grounded on their own sense of what is really important or of value. People are called upon to be true to themselves and to seek their own self-fulfillment. What this consists of, each must, in the last instance, determine for him-or herself. No one else can or should try to dictate its content.[35]

Taylor, a Roman Catholic, uses explicitly religious language to further explain that in the modern West, "Our moral salvation comes from recovering authentic moral contact with ourselves ."[36] He speaks of our individuality as a form of salvation. Where there is no longer a god to provide meaning, we must find it somewhere. Even Jesus acknowledged, "Man shall not live by bread alone."[37] We need some divine word to guide us and help us face our vulnerability.

In the vacuum of God's death, Nietzsche predicted that we would each have to become gods ourselves. He didn't imagine we would suddenly develop superpowers or demand others bow in worship to us. He reckoned we would have to find in ourselves what God had previously given us. God had long been our source of meaning, direction, and security.

Nietzsche recognized that now we would have to turn inward for those same answers. We are now responsible for searching our own hearts for that meaning and security. You might say that the individual imagination is now the only source of truth.

And that imagination has now been severed from any divine intervention.

A past Barna Group survey found that 91 percent of US adults agreed that "the best way to find yourself is by looking within yourself." They also found that 76 percent of practicing Christians agreed with that statement. That kind of consensus is astonishing. It's hard to imagine 91 percent of Americans agreeing about anything these days. Still, Barna found that 86 percent of US adults also agreed that "to be fulfilled in life, you should pursue the things you desire most," and 84 percent agreed that "the highest goal of life is to enjoy it as much as possible." David Kinnaman, president of the Barna Group, concluded, "The highest good, according to our society, is 'finding yourself' and then living by 'what's right for you.'" [38]

That advice has become a new kind of religious dogma for our culture, as heavily defended as any past religious claim. The Barna Group also found that 89 percent of US adults agreed that "people should not criticize someone else's life choices."[39] Again, 76 percent of practicing Christians agreed. According to our culture, you must look inside to find meaning, and when you find it, no one is allowed to question what you find.

As sociologist Robert Bellah explained in *Habits of the Heart*,

Anything that would violate our right to think for ourselves, judge for ourselves, make our own decisions, live our lives as we see fit, is not only morally wrong, it is sacrilegious. Our highest and noblest aspirations, not only for ourselves, but for those we care about, for our society and for the world, are closely linked to our individualism."[40]

There are now few offenses worse than questioning another person's individual moral judgments.

So, as the serpent has done since the garden, a voice whispers to us both an insecurity and a solution. The insecurity? You are living a diminished life. You haven't truly found yourself. With its traditions and obligations, this world is holding you back from who you could be. And so, the idol is also planted.

Our imaginations are encouraged to abandon any external expectation or wisdom. We're told to close our eyes and imagine whatever our hearts desire. Our salvation will be having the courage to pursue that.

It sounds modern, but it is not. It's the temptation of Eve that led to their fall. It's the temptation of Israel to cast a golden god to follow. It's the temptation of the Pharisees that blinded them by their own self-image. It's the temptation of Jane Eyre, by which her need for love eclipses what God was offering. It's the same internal mechanism by which insecurity unleashes the worst of our imagination toward making an image and idol of the heart.

It is the same obsession that has long blinded us. But the insecurity and the imagination, which produce idolatry, are still only the beginning of this inner mechanism of offense. Such temptations always begin with a thrilling rush of optimism and potential. Every trap has its bait. Every snare is disguised. But it is by this insecurity and idol imagination the machine begins and turns toward our destruction.

If unchecked, its churning will eventually produce symptoms in our lives. Where there is insecurity, there will be idolatry, and that idolatry will eventually lead to imitation, competition, and envy. Unchecked, left unoffended, the machine will claim more of your heart.

The obsession will grow worse. The blindness spreads. The insecurity worsens. The optimism gives way to frustration. We have reached into the trap, taken the bait. It won't be long before we feel its teeth digging in and the knot slipping tighter.

* * *

"What profit is an idol
when its maker has shaped it,
a metal image, a teacher of lies?
For its maker trusts in his own
creation when he makes speechless idols!"
— Habakkuk 2:18

CHAPTER 5

IMITATION: "WHO ARE YOU TO ASK ME?"

"A woman from Samaria came to draw water. Jesus said to her, 'Give me a drink.' ...The Samaritan woman said to him, 'How is it that you, a Jew, ask for a drink from me, a woman of Samaria?'"

JOHN 4:7, 9

"If we listen to Satan, who may sound like a very progressive and likeable educator, we may feel initially that we are 'liberated,' but this impression does not last because Satan deprives us of everything that protects us from rivalistic imitation. Rather than warning us of the trap that awaits us, Satan makes us fall into it."

RENÉ GIRARD[1]

They were passing by Sychar in Samaria. It was the sixth hour, sometime around noon. Jesus was weary from his travels. He sent his disciples ahead to find food. Knowing the place's significance, he decided to sit and rest alone. He was near the field Jacob had long ago given to his son Joseph.[2] Jacob, the father of twelve sons who would become the twelve tribes of Israel. It was a place full of history and an ancient sense of identity. It was the kind of place where imitation went unnoticed, where imitation of the old arguments and debates would even be expected. And it was there that Jesus would have to risk offense to free one woman from the trap imitation always produces.

In that field was an equally old well. Jesus sat on its stone walls to rest. He was thirsty but had no means of drawing from the well. The Son of God, the Word by which the chaotic waters of Genesis had been separated and creation formed, found himself tired and thirsty and alone in a field, sitting on the rim of a well waiting. He would not have to wait long.

A lone Samaritan woman came to the well at the noon hour to draw water. Odd to find her alone. Strange to be drawing water in the heat of the day. And even more unusual, alarming even, for the two of them to strike up a conversation. A man and a woman meeting at a well floods the scene with echoes of Moses defending Zipporah, Isaacs's meeting Rebekah, even Jacob first seeing the beautiful Rachel. All had taken place at wells. But Jesus was not there to find a wife, and his conversation with the Samaritan woman quickly wandered, not into romance, but into controversy and offense. The history of that place served only to draw out further the tensions and controversies that divided them.

Jesus spoke first. "Give me a drink." At worst, it sounds abrupt, and the woman seemed shocked. But she was shocked to find Jesus speaking to her at all. "How is it that you, a Jew, ask for a drink from me, a woman of Samaria?" she answered.[3] It didn't take long for their conversation to fall into the ruts of their identities and the swirling religious and racial questions of their day. In case you are unfamiliar with the impropriety of Jesus's words, John, the gospel writer, adds the parenthetic detail that the Jews did not usually have any association with Samaritans. Jewish men didn't talk to Samaritan women. Not in towns, not on the road, not at wells, never alone. But Jesus did. The woman was understandably offended.

In his commentary on John, New Testament scholar Craig Keener acknowledges, "That Jesus talks with a woman, especially under such circumstances, probably appeared offensive." But it wasn't just their genders that made the conversation dangerous. Keener adds, "The greatest offense of the narrative, however, is the first one the woman picks up on: being a Jew, he especially should avoid talking with a Samaritan woman."[4] Their racial and religious differences were a major obstacle as well.

The woman didn't jump to fulfill Jesus's request. She didn't rush to get him water. Instead, she answered with her own question. "Who are you to ask me for a drink?" She turned to the well-worn lines of identity that divided and complicated both of their positions. He was a Jew and a man. She was a Samaritan and a woman. For her, those realities predefined the situation and their conversation. She, without thought, framed the moment in the stereotypes which characterized both their identities.

Jesus did not seem surprised by her objection or that she shifted the topic to their identities. He pressed the question of identity deeper. He answered her, saying, "If you knew the gift of God, and who it is that is saying to you, 'Give me a drink,' you would have asked him, and he would have given you living water."[5] She was right to ask who he was, but her question didn't go far enough; it only imitated the objections she knew from the world. Jesus wanted her to ask it from her own position of curiosity and need. Who they each were was a question that mattered far more than she realized.

Hers was the language of division, imitation, and conflict. But Jesus never imitated it. Jesus never addressed her as merely a Samaritan or a woman. "If you knew who I was," Jesus answered, "you would have asked me for a drink."[6] Her offense at Jesus's request and her imitation of a world divided by its predefined conflicts kept her from seeing the opportunity before her and from recognizing whom it was offending her. Jesus was prepared to give her water from a much deeper well. But she would have to see past the categories of imitation that defined her. She would have to recognize him as an individual; she would have to come to him as an individual as well.

The gift of Christ's hard words is that they possess the power to break apart our objections. They can also free us from the distorted imitations that trap us and put words in our mouth. Jesus risks offending you to offer you your true identity. We've already seen how identities can become idols through our search for a more secure self. Though we usually think we're imagining a unique version of ourselves, the truth is, idols are a form of imitation. We're not as original as we think. We search for security by imitating those who seem to possess it.

*　*　*

The ancient world had plenty of conflicting identities, each a form of imitation. Those categories and the divisions they created often appear in Scripture. From conflicts between the rich and powerful to the debates dividing Pharisees, Sadducees, and Essenes, the biblical world was fragmented by all kinds of divisions. The lines dividing a first-century Jewish teacher from a Samaritan woman living with a man who was not her husband weren't superficial. They were rigid and carried with them a long history of suspicion, animosity, and plenty of offense. Each of those identity markers would have been fixed and rarely transgressed. In the ancient world, your identity had very real consequences. It's worth observing each of the lines that divided Jesus and the Samaritan woman.

First, the division between Jews and Samaritans can be traced back to the Old Testament exiles. The region of Samaria had been conquered first by the Assyrians, who practiced a policy of forced assimilation through relocation. After conquering a nation, the Assyrians often relocated large portions of the population, making it difficult to maintain a social identity. They also flooded the conquered land with people from other places, mixing their population to dilute national identities.

The Jews from the southern kingdom of Judah, from whom Jesus traced his ancestry, were exiled later by the Babylonians and eventually allowed to return to Jerusalem under the rule of the Persian Empire. Many of the great stories of defiance, from Daniel in the lion's den to the three Jewish youths thrown into the fire, come from this period of exile and their effort to preserve their identity.

When the Jews eventually returned to their homeland, they found that many of their neighbors to the north, what was the northern kingdom of Israel, had intermarried with gentiles. And while still worshiping Israel's God, they had been shaped by the broader pagan culture relocated around them. The Samaritans dressed differently, read only from the Pentateuch, worshiped on a different mountain, and lived by a different calendar. That might not seem like a lot, but it was enough to cause tension. The returning Jews, many having suffered dramatically in exile, were quickly suspicious.

Learning of the Jews' plans to rebuild the temple in Jerusalem, the Samaritans sent a delegation to offer assistance, but the

Jews refused. Offended, the Samaritans responded by building their own temple on Mount Gerizim. This tension occasionally turned violent. In 128 BCE, fresh off the victory of overthrowing the Greek Seleucid kingdom, the Jews marched on Samaria and destroyed the Samaritan temple, burning it to the ground. By the time of Jesus, the animosity between Jews and Samaritans was a fixed part of life and geography. Biblical scholar Leon Morris concludes, "Occasions of friction were not lacking, and by New Testament times a settled attitude of hostility had resulted. At the time with which we are dealing the hostility between Jews and Samaritans was bitter and widespread."[7]

This dramatic question of where to worship quickly emerged in Jesus's conversation with the Samaritan woman. She asked Jesus which mountain, Jerusalem or Gerizim, was the correct place of worship. She was raising the question that had long divided them. You can't help but wonder if that question was really her own, or was it not the question long ago given to her. Even as she came to recognize Jesus's identity as a prophet, she still struggled to see past the conflict which separated and defined Jews from Samaritans. She blindly imitated and vocalized what was expected.

Next, there was the question of their differing genders. In the first-century world of the Jewish faith, men, and especially teachers, didn't casually engage in conversation with any woman who was not their wife or close relative. Keener explains,

> According to Jewish sages, Jewish men were to avoid unnecessary conversation with women. Thus among six activities listed as unbecoming for a scholar is conversing with a woman, and in theory, the strict opined that a wife could be divorced without her marriage settlement if she spoke with a man in the street.[8]

But Jesus did far more than just speak to a woman. He initiated a lengthy conversation and requested she provide him with water to drink. That meant he would have drunk from her utensils. He had none of his own, which she pointed out. She understood the impropriety of Jesus's conversation and the religious tension of his request. To share so many words with an unknown woman was risky; to drink from the unclean pail of a sinful Samaritan woman was far beyond the boundary lines. This contact would have left Jesus ceremonially unclean. Again, it was surprisingly the Samaritan woman who pointed out this obstacle between them.

Their conversation was full of offense. Each response seemed to transgress more social boundaries. When Jesus's disciples returned, they too were shocked to find him talking alone with her. They immediately understood the danger of the conversation. Jesus seemed to be the only one not scandalized by it.

Yet there is an important consistency to their conversation. The labels of identity and the language of conflict were always spoken by the woman. She brought up the lines which divided them. Read the passage carefully and you'll see it. She pointed out that he was a man and a Jew and that she was a Samaritan and a woman. She raised the question of defilement through contact. She raised the question of where to worship and the violent history between Jews and Samaritans. She struggled to grasp Jesus's answers, each time returning to the identities which predefined her world and self-understanding.

Jesus never once used her labels. He never once labeled her or reduced her to how they were each perceived by the world around them. Instead, Jesus spoke of God's gift, of living water, of eternal life, and of a coming hour when mountains wouldn't matter, but true worshipers would worship in spirit and truth. Jesus led her, stumbling over every obstacle of the world's identities, to a final and more profound question of identity. She admitted, "I know that Messiah is coming (he who is called Christ). When he comes, he will tell us all things." Jesus answered simply, "I who speak to you am he." [9] Jesus was interested in exploring only one identity. It was not hers nor those suggested by the world. The identity Jesus pressed her to recognize was his own.

CHRIST CALLS US AS INDIVIDUALS

Most commentators recognize that in John's gospel, the story of the Samaritan woman parallels the story that precedes it. [10] Before Jesus's conversation with the woman, he'd had a similarly private conversation with a Jewish teacher named Nicodemus. Unlike that isolated Samaritan woman, Nicodemus was one of the leading teachers of Israel. Nicodemus came to Jesus alone at night. His motives were not entirely clear. He may have been personally interested in Jesus. He acknowledged being impressed with Jesus's miracles and credited them to God's divine favor, but Nicodemus also referred to Jesus as "Rabbi." He understood Jesus to be merely a teacher. Like the Samaritan woman, Nicodemus spoke, not from his own soul, but in imitation of the wider world he inhabited.

Nicodemus's words feel rehearsed. He comes across as an ambassador or a spokesman. His opening words of respect feel like the opening of a negotiation. And if you read closely, Nicodemus never refers directly to himself as an individual. Instead, he speaks in the plural. "Rabbi, we know that you are a teacher come from God," [11] he explained.

His coming at night shrouded the whole conversation in a veil of secrecy. Perhaps he was there to try and arbitrate some peace between Jesus and the Pharisees he represented. He certainly had some agenda for coming to Jesus. But we will never know for sure because Jesus interrupted Nicodemus's opening preamble with what feels like a strange, off-topic statement. Jesus said suddenly, "Truly, truly, I say to you, unless one is born again he cannot see the kingdom of God."[12]

Nicodemus opened the conversation speaking for the group he represented—he used the pronoun we—but Jesus only addressed him as an individual. "Truly, I say to you," Jesus consistently responded. Jesus kept pushing Nicodemus deeper into a conversation about himself. Not interested in abstract questions about groups and opinions, Jesus was interested in Nicodemus's soul.

In his great work on Christian discipleship, *The Cost of Discipleship*, the German pastor Dietrich Bonhoeffer wrote:

> Through the call of Jesus men become individuals. Willy-nilly, they are compelled to decide, and that decision can only be made by themselves. It is no choice of their own that makes them individuals: it is Christ who makes them individuals by calling them. Every man is called separately, and must follow alone. But men are frightened of solitude, and they try to protect themselves from it by merging themselves in the society of their fellow-men and in their material environment. ... They are unwilling to stand alone before Jesus and to be compelled to decide with their eyes fixed on him alone.[13]

Idols always draw us into groups because, in the narrative of the group, we can hide any individual sense of insecurity. The group becomes a justification. It obscures our individual needs. But a real encounter with Jesus will not let us hide in impersonal labels. It will not let us mask our own needs with the needs of our day. It will not allow us to remain hidden in the group. We are not permitted to go on imitating what we have seen and heard. When Christ calls us, he calls us out of the group. How many times did Jesus recognize a single individual amongst the crowd: the woman who touched his hem, Zacchaeus hanging from a limb, the lame man on his mat by the pool, Peter scrubbing his nets amongst the crowd? The Gospels are littered with the names and lives of individuals. Jesus saw them and spoke to them as individuals. He does the same with you.

Stepping out of our identity markers to stand alone before Christ doesn't erase our differences. God may call us as individuals, but he also created us in a particular place and within particular communities and groups. The New Testament church was also full of these divisions: debates about gender, race, and equality. Yet the apostle Paul could write things like, "There is neither Jew nor Greek, there is neither slave nor free, there is no male and female, for you are all one in Christ Jesus."[14]

But there certainly were still slaves and masters. Christ does not erase the biology of gender, nor immediately free the poor from economic bondage. Instead, the Gospels routinely depict encounters with Jesus so shockingly personal that they rework a person's identity. In the Gospels, Jesus spoke hard words that exposed individual lives, but in that new individuality, he also offered a personal word from God. As the prophet Isaiah expressed it when encountering God for himself, "Woe is me, for I am undone!"[15] In that undoing, you are born again.

Jesus's disinterest in your group and his focus on you as an individual can feel dismissive. You may be used to defining yourself by the group you belong to. Having formed your identity by the world's labels, Jesus's call to become a true individual can feel at first like he is diminishing your identity. Jesus's disinterest in your language and distinctions can feel like he is dismissing you. But he is not. He is taking you more seriously than you take yourself.

As hard as those conversations are, Jesus was not interested in Nicodemus or the Samaritan woman as abstract examples of the social groups they represented. Jesus was interested in them as individuals. Forcing us to let go of imitation often requires a hard word. We often need someone to expose our conformity to this world to have any chance of overcoming it. But the power of imitation, which binds us to the world, is not easily broken.

THE ROMANTIC LIE OF IMITATION

For all our talk about our heart's desires, we seem awkwardly ill-informed about where desire comes from and suspiciously confident that our hearts can be trusted. We live in a world that laughs at the idea of an external god who can speak, but we somehow find it perfectly plausible that each of us has an inner voice that guides us toward a truer version of ourselves. We think what our hearts want makes us unique. We trust desire to define our identity. But what if desire is just another form of hopeless imitation?

René Girard went so far as to call our inner voice of desire the "Romantic lie."[16] It is not even our own voice; it's always the voice of another. Girard understood desire and recognized that though we have come to place all our hopes upon our heart's desires, the real source of desire is the same as it's always been—imitation. Our desires are not actually our own.

Girard, a faithful Roman Catholic, was often called a polymath, a thinker whose ideas broke traditional academic boundaries. Trained as a historian and French literary critic, Girard's work expanded into philosophy, anthropology, and religion. But at the core of his work was a curiosity about the source of desire. Why do we want what we want? Are our desires our own?

Girard was born in France, where he lived through the German Nazi occupation as a student in Paris. In 1947, he came to the United States and worked at several universities, eventually ending his career at Stanford. He witnessed the rise of our identity-focused culture firsthand, but he had his own theory for how our heart's desires are formed. His ideas came to be known as the theory of mimetic desire.

Girard suggested that human nature is fundamentally mimetic, meaning we imitate each other. We may imagine that our desires are unique, but Girard believed that we desire things because we see other people desiring them. Insecurity sends us looking for a solution. We see someone who seems to have overcome the insecurity plaguing us. We recognize the objects and desires they possess, so we begin to value and desire those same objects. We want what they have because we believe it will make us like them. They become a model for our desire. You see how naturally what we idolize creates new desires. Idols always produce imitation. Girard concluded, "Man is the creature who does not know what to desire, and he turns to others in order to make up his mind. We desire what others desire because we imitate their desires."[17]

Perhaps the most basic example of mimetic desire can be seen in children at play. Imagine two toddlers entering a room full of toys. The first toddler selects a toy and begins to play with it. The second toddler may look through the other toys, but, even in a room full of toys, you know which one they will want. There may be better toys, but seeing the other toddler enjoying that particular toy makes the second child want it alone. Their desire is shaped by the desire of the other. The toy becomes intensely desirable because it promises the same fun they've seen in the other child's possession.

You also know how this scenario inevitably plays out. The second child wobbles over and physically takes the toy from the first, making the first child now desire the toy even more. They retaliate. As you will see in later chapters, mimetic desires always lead to mimetic rivalry and conflict. It also leads to obsession and a blind, intensifying desire.

Imitation has always formed our heart's desires, but today we seem far less aware of it. You may even object that you aren't imitating anyone. You are authentic and original. After all, what previous generation has had the means of individual self-expression we now possess? But Girard prophetically warned,

> In our days its nature is hard to perceive because the most fervent imitation is the most vigorously denied. ... The romantic vaniteux [person of vanity] does not want to be anyone's disciple. He convinces himself that he is thoroughly original. ... We must not be fooled by these individualisms professed with fanfare, for they merely hide a new form of imitation.[18]

Girard recognized that even the desire for originality can become a kind of imitation.

You can see this faux originality everywhere. If you look closely enough, you can also see the copying and the insecurity driving it. Why does every rebellious teenager who wants to overthrow social norms dress like every other teenager trying to overthrow social norms? Brands constantly present themselves as nonconforming, even as they sell millions of consumers the same products. No woman wants to show up to a party in the same dress as another, but she is happy to take fashion advice from a model wearing it on Instagram. The more your insecurity compels you to imitate, the more desperate you become to pass it off as originality. It is as the eighteenth-century scientist Georg Christoph Lichtenberg concluded, "To do the opposite of something is also a form of imitation, namely an imitation of its opposite."[19]

Might this hidden mechanism of imitation stirring and forming desires just beneath our awareness be contributing to one of the emerging complaints of modern life: the sense that we are each an imposter? According to a 2021 report by the American Psychological Association, as many as 82 percent of Americans now report deep feelings of insecurity about being a fraud.[20] Psychologists have labeled it the Imposter Phenomenon, unaware of its root cause. We have never placed more trust in our heart's desires, yet it seems we have never felt so little like ourselves.

Luke Burgis, author of *Wanting: The Power of Mimetic Desire in Everyday Life*, explains, "We are tantalized by models who suggest a desire for things that we don't currently have, especially things that appear just out of reach. The greater the obstacle, the greater the attraction."[21] Or you might say, the greater the insecurity, the greater the desire. That still, small voice speaking to you from within is more likely to be the voice of insecure desperation than it is your true authentic self. As Burgis correctly identifies, our "models are, in many cases, a person's secret idol."[22]

Seeing this imitation and insecurity in the Samaritan woman at the well is ironic. She was alone, perhaps even ostracized from her community, but still, she could not let go of the labels and imitations her community had taught her. She had no language for who she was beyond what the world had given her. Jesus alone offered her something new. Jesus alone was original. As difficult as it was, he called her out of the imitation and offered her living water to quench her deepest thirsts. Surely something in her long line of broken relationships pointed to the desire and thirst still unsatisfied by the world.

So too, our idols drive us by insecurity into idolatry and imitation. The imitation feels to us like a legitimate desire. For some, the desire might be career oriented; for others, it may be an image of an ideal family, a place you'd like to live, or maybe just a sense of personal independence. Those identities, and the desires that form them, are not original to you. They are a mash-up of online influencers, cultural celebrities, media personalities, and probably your friends' social media highlight reels. You see their success and begin to desire what they possess to try and cure your insecurities. You do this naturally and usually without much self-awareness. The only thing you recognize is that growing feeling of desire and desperation that you imagine is your own.

Girard recognized mimetic desire everywhere, in all the great works of literature and the desires of everyday life. But he also saw this practice of imitation at the center of the Bible. A student of Girard, Gil Bailie, observed that the original temptation of Eve involved exactly the mechanism of desire Girard observed elsewhere. An inner voice didn't awaken Eve's desire for the fruit. The fruit's desirability was suggested to her. The serpent modeled its desirability and pointed to the possibility of her becoming like God through eating it.

Eve's insecure need to know more, and the serpent's whispered promise, made the fruit desirable. Eve ate the fruit to become like God, even as she rebelled against him. Her desire was not her own. She was imitating it. The fruit promised to enlighten her, to make her more herself, but by that new desire, she and Adam became less who they really were. Is it not now obvious to all reading the story that the desire whispered by the serpent was a lie? But seeing it in the story and recognizing it in your heart are quite different.

THE SERPENT STILL WHISPERS

The idea of mimetic desire may only be philosophical to you but not to those exploiting it. Our society routinely trades on our insecurities. Imitation is the currency of our world. Learn to recognize the mechanics of mimetic desire, and you'll soon recognize it everywhere. After all, what is social media but a mimetic machine specifically designed to present you with models and desires, awakening in you constantly new insecurities, suggestions, and needs? But those platforms are just the beginning.

Today's digital algorithms know more about you and your deepest desires than you probably know about yourself. The algorithm has become a catalog of your most exploitable insecurities. They know what you search and what catches your eye. They understand what most motivates your behavior. The algorithms know what you desire and how to create new desires in you. Neil Postman, writing about modern changes in technology and marketing, candidly confessed, "What the advertiser needs to know is not what is right about the product but what is wrong about the buyer."[23]

If you picked up a magazine in the early 1900s, most ads were for common household goods, and most of the marketing copy was designed to sell you on features. This gadget could do it faster. This product costs less. This one came with a revolutionary new feature. Rarely do you see ads like those today. In 1927, writing for the *Harvard Review*, Paul Mazur, a Wall Street banker, predicted exactly what would occur. He wrote, "We must shift America from a needs to a desires culture." Today's marketers are keenly aware of their power to leverage your insecurity and offer you a model to solve it. They know how to create a desire that produces mindless imitation.

Recently I saw a commercial for a new Alfa Romeo luxury SUV. Only about a third of the commercial actually showed the vehicle. The other scenes were a montage of beautiful people, mansions, and pools, alluring landscapes with roads switch-backing through Italian hills—each perfectly cast in the mystery of shifting shadows and camera movements that made the images disappear as quickly as they were perceived, all of it passing like a dream. The voice-over whispered in a breathy narration, "When you look for things, when you search the polished showrooms, the markets, the runway shows, you are looking for me. ... And when you dream, when you dream of an SUV existing far beyond the ordinary, an SUV steeped in performance, infused with passion, artistic beyond description, you unknowingly dream of me. I am the end of your search, your drive, your dream. I am what you live for. I am Alfa Romeo Stelvio."[24]

Remember that the marketers who wrote that script were tasked with selling you a car. But they say almost nothing about the actual vehicle. Instead, they paint an image of the kind of person who might already own one and then suggest to your insecurity that you could be like them. They create a triangle of desire: you with your insecurities, a model who clearly has whatever it is you lack, and a product by which you might become like them. It's no coincidence that our culture so often speaks of influencers, models, and even American idols.

So, they speak of what "you unknowingly dream of." They aren't talking about a car anymore; they are talking about your insecurity. They, like the serpent, are whispering a desire. "Buy this car, and you will finally know who you are." You will find what you have been looking for.

You may not be in Alfa Romeo's target market for an SUV, or their ad might strike you as ridiculous, but someone is whispering to your insecurities: the perfect body, the thrill of distant adventure, the admiration of your peers, a sense of confidence or entrepreneurial success, maybe just a place to relax that is all your own. Alfa Romeo, Carhartt, Nike, Stanley, CrossFit, or Louis Vuitton. You got those desires from somewhere.

Why do you think brands like Nike dole out millions of dollars in athletic sponsorships, from Michael Jordan to Tiger Woods? Seeing a poster of Jordan holding a sneaker doesn't tell you anything about the shoe's flexibility or strength, but Michael Jordan holding the shoe suggests something much more important to you. If athletics shapes your identity, then this shoe will get you one step closer to that ideal self-image and the security you hope will come with it. If your deepest desire is to be the best, you need what the best already have. So, you are taught to imitate desire. If Michael Jordan wants it, you'll want it.

Most of us are sophisticated enough to realize buying Air Jordans doesn't mean you'll suddenly develop new athletic ability, but the nagging of your insecurities makes even the subtlest benefit worth the cost. Maybe the shoes won't help you dunk a basketball, but if putting them on makes you look or, more importantly, feel like someone who could, it's at least a start. It's at least a cheap trick to quiet the nagging of self-doubt. Maybe others will believe it—maybe you'll believe it too. Day after day, commercial after commercial, your deepest desires are shaped by the imitation of these models—whispers that exploit your insecurities.

Do you see the trap set in motion? The serpent prods your insecurity. That insecurity sends you searching for a solution, for salvation, for an idol. You find that idol in the example of another who seems more secure. So, you begin to imitate them. You take up their narrative, language, and identity. When asked, you speak exactly the words they've put into your mouth. You lose yourself just as you imagine you're finding yourself. The insecurity and the obsession over your insecurity only grow worse. Something has to shock you out of your decline.

EVERYTHING I EVER DID

It took a hard, offensive conversation for Jesus to free the Samaritan woman from her language of imitation. But as he revealed more of who he was, the layers of her imitations began to fall away. The real power of Jesus's conversation with the Samaritan woman came in her final transformation. She overcame the obstacle of Jesus's words and was changed by them. Though Jesus risked offending her, she did not leave offended. Instead, she followed the conversation and overcame their division to recognize both what Jesus was saying and who he was.

Jesus was no longer just a Jewish man with an unreasonable request. Jesus was the Messiah. That realization dramatically re-worked not only her sense of who Jesus was but also who she was. By his leading, she found herself exposed as an individual before him. By shedding her old identity and the imitations that formed it, she took up a new one.

Realizing who Jesus was, she abandoned her water jar and the work she had come to do. She rushed back into town and spoke to everyone, "Come, see a man who told me all that I ever did." It was a strange but paradoxically true response to encountering the offense of Christ. When asked to fetch her husband, she confessed to Jesus that she did not have one. Jesus added prophetically that the man she was living with was, in fact, also not her husband, but she had been married five times previously. Eventually, conversations with Jesus always push down into the real insecurities we try desperately to ignore.

The Samaritans were a highly religious society. Many commentators have speculated that she was alone at the well for precisely that reason. Her lifestyle and history with men had left her alienated from polite company. While she admitted it was true, her marital history was not something she was motivated to bring up on her own. Still, Jesus drew her attention to it. And suddenly, we find her running through the town, acknowledging that Jesus had exposed everything she had ever done. That deep insecurity driving so much of her desire, hidden in her imitation, once exposed, became her testimony.

She now ran through the town confessing what had just that morning ostracized her. "Come see a man who knew all about my past sins."[25] I don't think it was just Jesus's prophetic abilities that impressed her. Jesus was willing to offer her salvation, living water, even knowing who she was. Jesus knew her. Could she say that about any of the people or men who had populated her life? How many of us can say we are really known or that our deepest insecurities and imitations are known? We play the parts we're expected to. We raise the questions we've been taught to. We object where people like us are supposed to object. But Jesus wouldn't play along. He exposed her with a hard word, but in that exposed gap, he offered her real salvation. She would never thirst again.

She found in Jesus precisely what our pursuit of identity always fails to provide. She felt recognized, maybe for the first time in a long time. That is the paradox of Christ's calling. The only way to receive him is to abandon your identity. You must step out from the group that defines you and place yourself before him as an individual. You must drop the labels of this world: slave and master, male and female, Jew and gentile.

You don't cease to be those things, but you must break with your blind imitation of the world. Each is for Christ alone to define. Your imitation of the world will only diminish who you are. You must receive Christ alone. But when you do, he offers you a new identity. You will find a sense of identity greater than any labels could provide.

Jesus's call to death is always a promise of new life. Consider Jesus's words to his disciples again: "If anyone would come after me, let him deny himself and take up his cross and follow me. For whoever would save his life will lose it, but whoever loses his life for my sake will find it."[26]

It is equally true for your identity. Whoever clings to an identity, a group, a self-definition will lose it. It will diminish you and leave you thirsty. You will find a world constantly dividing and shrinking. You will wear yourself out in a life of endless imitation. You will never really know who you are. But for those willing to come to Christ alone, you will have it all given back to you in an even greater reward. You will be given living water and will never thirst again.

You discover who you are only by being willing to sacrifice who you think you are—and often who the world says you are. You find it in placing yourself before Christ. You find it in discovering who he is. It will come as an offense. He will ask you to step out from the crowd. He will require you to come alone. He will call you by your name, not by your associations. He may even offend those labels you've long trusted for your identity, but if you avoid being offended, he will offer you something far better. He will offer you himself. And you will recognize who you truly are in ways this world, with its competition and insecurities, never can.

For those unwilling to hear Jesus's hard words, for those who cannot overcome the offense of his revelation, they slip further into the trap. They go away offended and still blind. They cling to their idols and wallow in their insecurity. They cannot give up their imitation of the world. So, they will soon feel the true desperation of their condition. Their relentless imitation will make them desperate for affirmation, increasingly envious, and increasingly sensitive to the smallest offense.

* * *

"If then you have been raised with Christ, seek the things that are above, where Christ is, seated at the right hand of God. Set your minds on things that are above, not on things that are on earth. For you have died, and your life is hidden with Christ in God." — Colossians 3:1–3

CHAPTER 6

AFFIRMATION: "WOMAN, WHAT IS IT TO ME?"

"And Jesus said to her, 'Woman, what does this have to do with me? My hour has not yet come.' His mother said to the servants, 'Do whatever he tells you.'"

JOHN 2:4–5

"Surely you know that if a man can't be cured of churchgoing, the next best thing is to send him all over the neighbourhood looking for the church that 'suits' him until he becomes a taster or connoisseur of churches.… The search for a 'suitable' church makes the man a critic where the Enemy wants him to be a pupil."

C. S. LEWIS, THE SCREWTAPE LETTERS[1]

It was a strange way for a messiah to start a ministry that would be recognized for its divine healing, exorcism, and raising the dead. That Jesus's first miracle came in the backroom of a wedding, motivated by a potentially embarrassing social oversight, is not what you might expect. Jesus turned the water into wine, saved the party, and began counting down the clock to his final hour, but at the center of that story is also a strange conversation with his own mother and a lesson about Jesus's willingness to speak hard words to even those closest to him.

Traveling to Cana, Jesus had already begun gathering disciples, but at that early time, few recognized the trajectory of his ministry. Cana was not far from Jesus's hometown of Nazareth. The wedding party may have been close to Jesus's family, perhaps even relatives. First-century weddings were not like the social gatherings of today's ceremonies. Jewish weddings were multi-day feasts, often lasting as long as a week. With guests arriving from out of town, the host family was expected to provide for their needs throughout the festivities. It was a part of the larger emphasis on hospitality common in the ancient Middle East.

Mary, Jesus's mother, must have been close with the family because, on the third day, she learned that the wine had already run out. Somehow, she learned the news even before the wedding party. Word had not yet spread, and Mary seemed to have whispered it to Jesus in a side conversation. "They have no wine,"[2] she told him. She recognized it was about to get awkward.

Even today, running out of food or drinks at a party is an embarrassment, but in that ancient culture, the humiliation was much more significant. The Jewish Talmud includes a long list of various forms of theft. It had obvious examples but also included warnings against any man "who presses his fellow to come as his guest but does not intend to receive him properly."[3] The Talmud considered unpreparedness a form of thievery. The groom and his family had not prepared to support those they had invited, those who had come with an expectation of being supported. It was awkward, embarrassing, and dishonoring, a serious offense in the ancient world. Mary knew things were about to go bad. So, naturally, she took her concerns to her son.

In the scheme of Christ's agenda, it's a remarkably pedestrian moment. Jesus, the Savior of the world, and Mary, the mother of God, stood in the corner whispering about the dwindling supplies of a local party. What about the wine? But Jesus's response to his mother charged the situation with a new layer of complexity—and a new potential for offense.

Jesus answered his mother, "Woman, what does this have to do with me? My hour has not yet come."[4] Though modern translations often smooth out Jesus's response, a careful reader can't help but sense Jesus's escalation of the situation. Mary whispered a social dilemma, and Jesus responded with talk of his final hour. The two perceived the moment from very different perspectives.

Was Jesus annoyed with his mother's request? Maybe just melodramatic? And what of his obligation to honor his father and mother? Is this how the sinless son speaks to his own mother? Whatever his intention, it might surprise you that this wasn't the first time Jesus responded in such a way. As a child, Jesus had gone missing in Jerusalem. His parents searched desperately to find him. Eventually, they discovered him in the temple discussing the law with the scribes. With all Jerusalem before him, who would have expected a young boy to have wandered his way into the temple?

They did what every parent who has ever lost sight of their child does upon finding them: they hugged him and scolded him. I imagine Mary knelt before Jesus to get eye-to-eye, her hands on his shoulders. Mary charged, "Son, why have you treated us so? Behold, your father and I have been searching for you in great distress."[5] Again, Jesus's answer seemed strange. He responded, "Why were you looking for me? Did you not know that I must be in my Father's house?"[6]

His answer carried the same strange distancing it did that day in Cana, and the same potential for offense. Why? Jesus spoke with a distance that complicated the relationship between himself and his parents. Hearing the young boy's answer, Luke records that Mary and Joseph "did not understand the saying that he spoke to them." Jesus, in response, went with them and "was submissive to them."[7] Scripture says Mary treasured that strange conversation in her heart. She pondered it. She struggled to understand it.

How remarkable it must have been to raise a boy Mary knew would one day be the world's Savior. But Jesus's sinless life did not make the situation easier to grasp. There was between them an ongoing question of their relationship. What would it mean for Jesus to be both Son and Savior? What would it mean for his hour to come? What did he alone carry? And what would it mean for her to one day accept him as her Savior and Lord?

The goodness of the gospel is that we are welcomed into a new relationship with God. We are welcomed into the love of a Savior who would give his life for us. But do not mistake that relational invitation for one of cheap or easy approval. Jesus comes to show us love, which is not the same as affirmation. In fact, our distorted need for affirmation can actually keep us from Jesus and his real love. That was a topic Jesus was not afraid to raise, neither with his mother nor his followers. Jesus spoke perhaps his most offensive words on precisely this topic: our need for relationships and our need to be affirmed by them.

* * *

In a 1960 interview with *The Paris Review*, poet Robert Frost explained, "Families break up when people take hints you don't intend and miss hints you do intend."[8] Jesus's conversation with his mother broke the social script and probably her expectations. It came with risk, but Jesus had a point to make.

As we have seen Jesus repeatedly do, he used offense as a test. There would be no flattery nor platitudes. He was no yes-man. Jesus placed an obstacle in Mary's path to reveal her desires and to draw out a question of their relationship. He risked offending her. The New Testament commentator Craig Keener explained, "Jesus creates an obstacle partly to challenge her to greater faith."[9]

First, he addressed her as woman instead of mother.[10] Much effort has been made to smooth out Jesus's words and to remove their potential for offense. The NIV goes so far as to change Jesus's words from woman to "dear woman." It sounds strange to our modern ears to hear a man address any woman by that title, but it was not a sign of disrespect in the ancient world. Addressing an individual as woman was similar to calling someone ma'am. It's not offensive that Jesus would use the title, but using woman for one's own mother was strange.

The New Testament scholar Leon Morris writes, "There appear to be no examples of this use cited other than those in this Gospel. It is neither a Hebrew nor a Greek practice. That Jesus calls Mary 'Woman' and not 'Mother' probably indicates that there is a new relationship between them as he enters his public ministry."[11] Keener also recognizes this change, writing, "Jesus is establishing a degree of distance between himself and his mother. . . . She approached him not as her son but as a miracle worker; he replies not as her son but as her Lord."[12]

Mary came to her son with a social dilemma. She seemed to imply he might intervene. She appealed to his power, and he responded in direct proportion. His power was his, not hers. He was her son, but he was much more. His intentional word of distance forced her to consider her own motives for the request. But Jesus made that point clearer.

Jesus added, "What does this have to do with me?" [13] Here the translations become even more intrusive. The Greek is very simple. If translated literally, it would read, "What of me and you?" It was a familiar idiom common to the Gospels but unexpected in this context. Wherever the phrase is used, it denotes a degree of distance and even hostility. In the Gospels, it's repeatedly used when Jesus encountered the demonic. For example, in Luke 8, a demon-possessed man came and fell at Jesus's feet. He cried out in a loud voice, "What have you to do with me, Jesus, Son of the Most High God?"[14]

Translators tell us that the phrase usually denotes open hostility or a reluctance to become involved in a disputed matter. Yet, it seems to be this very ambiguity Jesus sought to employ. His question forced Mary to interpret the situation no longer by her request but by who Jesus was and his purpose. What would it mean for him to intervene? What had he come to do? What would it cost him?

Placing distance between their relationship as mother and son and forcing Mary to consider this ambiguous question of purpose was a test. This was an obstacle she would either recognize or stumble over. Jesus's abrupt response tested her ability to see beyond the expectations of their relationship and even the uncomfortable situation of the moment. It forced her to set aside those expectations and consider her son as her sovereign Lord. Jesus's reply, as usual, was fundamentally a question of discipleship. He was asking her to place her expectations, desires, and relationships under his lordship—all at the risk of offense.

Jesus made this request not only of his mother, but he made it of all his disciples. Jesus asked his followers to set aside the priority of their existing relationships to receive him first. They are some of Jesus's strongest words. Luke records that as the crowds built around him, Jesus turned and said to them, "If anyone comes to me and does not hate his own father and mother and wife and children and brothers and sisters, yes, and even his own life, he cannot be my disciple."[15]

In Matthew's gospel, Jesus's mother and brothers tried to reach him through a crowded house. Jesus was told his family was outside trying to get his attention. Jesus responded, "Who is my mother, and who are my brothers?" He gestured toward his disciples seated around him and answered, "Here are my mother and my brothers! For whoever does the will of my Father in heaven is my brother and sister and mother."[16]

However, the Scriptures are not hostile to earthly relationships. The Ten Commandments include the honoring of parents. Marriage is equated with Christ's own love for the church. Believers are instructed to love neighbors and enemies as themselves. We are encouraged to form friendships modeled on the relationships of brotherhood and sisterhood.

You can't read Scripture without recognizing the remarkable priority of relationships, and yet Jesus repeatedly seems to place an obstacle in the path of our relational pursuits. He forces a peculiar distance which, in its most charged and intensive comparison, he equates to hate. What is that distance Jesus forces into our relationships, even into his relationship with his own mother? What did he recognize about our relationships that were prone to keep us from being his true disciples?

If we are not careful, our earthly relationships can replace God. More specifically, the affirmation we seek from those relationships can mask our insecurities and legitimize our desires. Relationships can become an obstacle to recognizing the insecurity and idolatry in our hearts. Imitation can't solve our sense of insecurity. Usually, it worsens the insecurity. Wherever there is imitation, there will be a growing desperation for affirmation. We need others to affirm what we're trying. We need affirmation to convince ourselves it's working. That impulse is old.

It's no surprise that having taken the forbidden fruit, Eve passed it to Adam. He shared with her in that act of rebellion, their mutual participation offering them each the affirming confidence of their action. Their relationship offered mutual justification for their disobedience. They affirmed each other's idolatrous choice. Jesus understood the danger. We surround ourselves with people who tell us what we want to hear. We retreat into the comfortable identities our relationships offer. We also accept Jesus as long as he too lifts us up. But we are not ready to walk away from our sources of affirmation, and we are not ready to listen to a Savior who exposes hard things. The people of Isaiah's day pleaded with him, "Do not prophesy to us what is right; speak to us smooth things, prophesy illusions."[17] They did not want hard words; we want prophets who will affirm what they already believe. They wanted to hear things that were easy to accept.

Seeking affirmation from others is the natural result of the mechanism of offense at work in the human heart. Insecurity leads to idolatry. Idolatry produces blind imitation. Imitation leaves us uncertain and still insecure. So, we go looking for people who will offer us the affirmation we crave. Tell me I'm good. Tell me my identity is valuable. Tell me I'm making progress. We're willing to rework even our relationship with God into one of these voices of affirmation. How much of Christian ministry has now become a priesthood of affirmation and a God who only says smooth things? We demand a God who will give us what we want, and what we want is our own affirmation.

A WORLD IN NEED OF AFFIRMATION

In 427 CE, one of the church's most influential leaders, Augustine, described the growing threats of the church in his day. Christians pleaded, "Let those who are over us only prescribe to us what we ought to do, and pray for us that we may do it; but let them not rebuke and censure us if we should not do it." Augustine answered, "You must be rebuked even for that very reason that you do not wish to be rebuked. For you do not wish that your faults should be pointed out to you; you do not wish that they should be touched, and that such a useful pain should be caused you that you may seek the Physician."[18] It's worth noting that Augustine was addressing those already in the church, and even they didn't like being disagreed with or challenged with any difficult word.

The church has long been tempted by that fashionable logic of every age: give the people what they want. The modern church growth movement has made us experts at that, but even the old crowns of ancient power knew the lesson. Give the mob bread and circus and you can do just about anything else you want. Affirm the people and they will affirm you.

The apostle Paul often saw this temptation in the early church. For instance, he placed the young minister Timothy in a very difficult assignment in Ephesus, a major metropolitan city in the ancient world, with plenty of the trendiest pagan religions. The church in Ephesus was constantly being sucked into the controversies of Ephesian culture, often swirling around gender and competing mythologies. Paul encouraged Timothy to step into his new role as a pastor with clarity and conviction. He wrote to Timothy, "Preach the word; be prepared in season and out of season; correct, rebuke and encourage—with great patience and careful instruction." But Paul also recognized not everyone would listen. He went on to explain, "For the time will come when people will not put up with sound doctrine. Instead, to suit their own desires, they will gather around them a great number of teachers to say what their itching ears want to hear."[19]

Are we aware of this tendency in ourselves? The church today panics over what it imagines to be the rising tide of secular atheism destined to wipe away Christendom. We scramble to construct defenses against disbelief and coming persecution. However, I think Paul better understood human nature and the consequences of our idolatry. Few completely denounce God or faith. Far more common is the gradual drift into self-interests and personal desires. We shift religion into whatever we want it to be. We theologize God into affirming whatever we need.

Paul recognized that the danger the church faced was not a single conflict that would split it in two; the church would instead fracture into its least common denominator—the self. Every person would become their own patched-together religion. For every desire, there would be some new voice with a clever logic of justification. The gospel would be drowned out, not in overpowering opposition but, as Neil Postman warned, "drowned in a sea of irrelevance."[20] Be it God, gurus, self-help books, or meditation prompts from a watch, we're happy for any spiritual idea that helps us get where we want to go. As Nietzsche's madman recognized, we now, out of our insecurity, invent our own religions. Religion has not disappeared from America, as so many feared; instead, it has, like everything from our entertainment to our diets, become personalized. Religion has shifted from the risk of offense to the affirmation of the self.

Sociologist Philip Rieff observed, "Religious man was born to be saved, psychological man is born to be pleased."[21] Rieff labeled this new search for personalized feelings of well-being the "triumph of the therapeutic." Writing in *The Culture of Narcissism*, Christopher Lasch, a student of Rieff, explains, "People today hunger not for personal salvation, let alone for the restoration of an earlier golden age, but for the feeling, the momentary illusion, of personal well-being, health, and psychic security."[22] Life is measured by feelings of happiness and self-actualization: self-care, self-help, and self-esteem.

To describe this new prioritization of feeling, philosopher Alasdair MacIntyre coined the phrase "emotivism," defining it as "the doctrine that all evaluative judgments and more specifically all moral judgments are nothing but expressions of preference, expressions of attitude or feeling."[23] When we call something good, we no longer mean it has inherited moral qualities of goodness recognizable to all; we now mean it makes us feel good.

Sunday after church, sitting at Applebee's with friends, you're far more likely to talk about how a sermon or worship song made you feel than to discuss its truthfulness. Consider how often we replace phrases like "I think that's true" with "I feel like that's true." But emotivism is also impacting the way we evaluate negative feelings. If a positive feeling is associated with being morally good, then an experience that produces negative feelings must be inherently bad. To make someone feel bad is often seen as morally wrong. Anything that risks a negative emotion must itself be negative. Our feelings become our sense of morality. Truth becomes what we feel. Faith is what makes us feel good.

I prefer the advice of pastor and author Eugene Peterson.

> Feelings are great liars. If Christians worshipped only when
> they felt like it, there would be precious little worship. We think
> that if we don't feel something, there can be no authenticity in
> doing it. But the wisdom of God says something different: that
> we can act ourselves into a new way of feeling much quicker
> than we can feel ourselves into a new way of acting.[24]

Far better to act upon truth and let our emotions be reshaped
than to be led solely by our emotions. But without a witness to the
truth, our world has been left to trust only what we feel.

Philip Rieff prophetically warned that while

> a wider range of people will have 'spiritual' concerns and en-
> gage in 'spiritual' pursuits. . . . The wisdom of the next social
> order, as I imagine it, would not reside in right doctrine, ad-
> ministered by the right men, who must be found, but rather
> in doctrines amounting to permission for each man to live an
> experimental life.[25]

We will no longer look for those willing to correct us. We will only
look for those willing to offer us the affirmation of what we feel.

In *The Rise and Triumph of the Modern Self*, Carl Trueman, a college professor, explains how the church has been impacted. He argues,

> Our major problems are defined using the categories of happi-
> ness and contentment, not those of guilt and forgiveness. That
> is why we now get Christian books on slimming, on better sex,

on learning to love ourselves more. God has been sentimentalised and the human predicament has been trivialised to the point where Christianity is seen to centre on the problem of a marred self-image, not a marred divine image. The idea that God is angry with sin, that our problem is, first and foremost, that of alienation from our creator rather than alienation from self, scarcely seems to feature.[26]

Many churches have become safe places not for exploring the counter-cultural truths of Christ but for exploring your own life and spiritual pursuits. Trueman observes a connection between how the therapeutic culture has impacted educational spaces and our churches. He writes,

> Our institutions, particularly our voluntary institutions, are more like boutiques competing for customers in the marketplace of self-fulfillment. Colleges sell themselves on the basis of allowing students to find themselves and reach their potential. And churches promote their programs as sources of personal happiness and well-being.[27]

Consider a recent poll reported in Time Magazine.[28] Sixty-six percent of American women and 54 percent of American men believe that self-improvement is the path to accomplishing good in the world. What kind of self-improvement? Thirty-five percent said they would turn to a place of worship, while 34 percent said they would go to the gym. Both are now legitimate answers. Each person must find their own forms of meaning, a church service or a morning workout group; the choice is now yours. And all choices should be affirmed.

IF ONLY WE COULD BE MORE RELEVANT

How should a church respond to such changes? How do you share the gospel with a distracted and self-focused crowd? Good intentions have moved the church into the therapeutic. We have been trying to meet people at their recognized places of need. How else can you get them to listen? We have been trying to remain relevant to those needs most pressing to modern individuals. But perhaps attempting to stay relevant has been the greatest mistake the church has made in this world. For being relevant may have robbed us of the most important distinctions we were called to preach. Being relevant has led us to forfeit Christ's hard words and the real power of change they contain.

When I went to seminary, few topics seemed as critical to our time as cultural relevance. It would be our way forward. We were convinced we needed to rework our worship services, sermons, and discipleship processes to better relate to the new postmodern world we now serve.

I took a course in seminary on pastoral leadership, which was all about connecting with the unchurched. The course culminated in a final project in which we designed material for a church plant in a secular city. I was surprised when my paper was returned with a grade of a B-. Digging through the professor's notes, I found he had circled several words like gospel, church, and sermon, leaving the explanation that these words no longer had meaning in a secular community and, worse, might be triggering to the de-churched. He suggested I find more contextualized words for the people I sought to reach.

At the time, I assumed he was right, but I have thought about that assignment for years, and I am increasingly convinced it's exactly where we all went wrong. We imagined that for someone to encounter Christ, they had to first like the church. They have to enjoy being with us before they can imagine enjoying being with Christ. We imagined that they were only interested in hearing from people like themselves. We imagined that if we could repackage Jesus as the answer to the questions they were already asking and use the same words they spoke, it would draw them in. We amplified Jesus's words of affirmation and minimized those that risked offense.

We made the church and Jesus so relevant it lost its ability to say anything contradictory to the world. Our lives became indistinguishable from our neighbors, and our words about God and salvation took on the language of daytime talk shows and self-help gurus. Afraid of offending, we drained the gospel of its power to confront. We abandoned the language of repentance and the Jesus that contradicts, and we took up the mantel of therapy. We peddled Christian doctrine as self-help remedies to a better marriage, finances, and workplace purpose. At its worst, we allowed the evaluations of an unbelieving culture to become the measuring stick for the church's truth.

Many churches publicly display on their signs and marketing material that they are welcoming and affirming. Usually, the phrase is meant to communicate a particular theological position related to sexuality, but I think our need for affirmation runs much deeper. We're all looking for it. We want to find churches that "work for us." Services that help us feel better about ourselves and preachers with advice on how to get more out of life, the life we've already built in our heart's desires. We want a priesthood of affirmation, a message of self-improvement, and a God of encouragement.

While it's easy to blame the church for this drift toward religious therapeutics, a much better question is, how has it impacted the way you follow Jesus and how you think about your faith? Do you still have room for offense? How about a savior of offense? Do you still have a view of God large enough to challenge you, to frustrate you, even offend you, if that's what it takes?

You may still read the Bible, listen to Christian music, collect your favorite Christian podcasts and sermon series, but are you still looking for God? Or has your faith turned into a search for permission and affirmation? I bet if you pay close attention, you'll find plenty of evidence of the therapeutic in your own life as well.

John's gospel may not give us enough to speculate on Mary's inner thoughts about the party's wine, but we do know enough to recognize the temptation. How easily, even standing next to the Savior of the world, our hearts turn to social standing, the potential for embarrassment, and the leveraging of relationships for our own affirmation.

Mary was not immune to insecurity or imitation or even the need to leverage her son's power to escape an awkward situation. But for Jesus, that day at Cana would prove to be about far more than wine and social standing. It would be the beginning of his end.

JESUS: HE GETS ME

The greatest consequence of our new therapeutic interest may be what it's done to our understanding of Christ. Focused on our desires, judging everything by our emotional experiences, and desperately searching for a deeper sense of personal fulfillment, Jesus easily becomes a kind of life coach ready to help encourage us when we're down and spur us to keep believing more in ourselves. Have you noticed how everyone seems to think Jesus is on their side? Everyone seems to imagine Jesus thinking and feeling just like they do. Liberals and conservatives, religious and irreligious, everyone points to Jesus as evidence for the veracity of their own views.

We want Jesus like we want a good friend: there when we need them, always ready with an encouraging word, always believing in us, happy to listen when we need to unload the day's drama, and if he can occasionally chip in an extra blessing or even a miracle for our help, all the better. Jesus becomes a buddy, a pal, a divine companion who must always look down with sympathy for our challenges. We imagine he hates what we hate, likes what we like, and generally gets frustrated by the same things we do. Jesus believes in us even when we struggle to believe in ourselves.

Perhaps you've seen "Buddy Christ," a parody of a Catholic icon.[29] It's a cartoonish figure of Jesus winking, pointing one hand at the onlooking crowd and giving a thumbs up with his other. Created to appear in a comical film, the icon was designed to replace the Catholic crucifix, which some find too depressing. It was a joke, but the figure has become a social trend, now produced as an action figure, bobblehead, and a popular online meme. To be fair, no one is actually worshipping this cartoon Jesus, but as parodies often hint at deeper truth, it may be closer to our image of Christ than most of us are willing to admit. For many, Christ is now formed in our image far more than we are formed into his. He is formed to be what we imagine we need. To say what we would like to hear said. And always ready to agree with the desires we find in our own hearts. Tim Keller was wise to warn, "If your god never disagrees with you, you might just be worshiping an idealized version of yourself."[30]

Many of these Christian therapeutic trends may contain elements of truth and may even be pragmatically helpful in growing a church. But, collectively, they reveal just how much our faith has come to focus on ourselves and how much of it is meant only to sooth our insecurities. Reworking faith to meet the psychological and therapeutic needs of our day, peddling happiness over salvation, we've robbed our faith of something crucial: its power to offend. The therapeutic and the offensive are incompatible. One seeks affirmation, the other reproof. The further the church slides into the therapeutic, the less it can speak Christ's word of offense, and the less it can save us from ourselves.

But God is not a wish dream. He is holy. A fire that consumes. A sword that divides. A voice that shatters. Our God is a living God, a God who, when encountered, led people to fall on their faces, caused them to cry out, and made them come undone. There are consequences to our reduction of faith: we have lost the greatness of God and with it the real goodness of his word. Goodness which, as Augustine points out, must first wound before it can fully heal.

We need to recover the offense of Christ and his gospel not as some weapon to wield against our lost culture. We need the offense of Christ to rescue us from ourselves and from the insecurity and affirmation that distorts desire. We need his offense to save us from the self-absorbed religious lives we're prone to collapse into. We need Jesus to offend us so that he might save us. And that is exactly what he came to do.

FAITH BEFORE FLESH

Once as Jesus walked with the crowd, a woman shouted, "Blessed is the womb that bore you, and the breasts at which you nursed!" Jesus turned and answered, "Blessed rather are those who hear the word of God and keep it!" [31]

Who wouldn't consider Mary blessed? What a position and honor to have been the mother of Jesus. But that earthly relationship was not enough. Having nursed the Son of God at her own breast was not enough to earn entrance into his kingdom. Earthly relationships can never fulfill eternal desires. Mary would have to receive Jesus as Lord too. It was a point Jesus made to his parents from the beginning.

Mary had received a great honor in bearing Christ, but it also came with a test. Mary faced all the same temptations we do. But her relational proximity to Jesus would have tested her ability to really follow him. When was the moment in which Mary shifted from caring for her son to submitting to him? When did Mary lay down all the imagined benefits of maternity for the cost of discipleship?

Augustine explained,

> Mary was more blessed in accepting the faith of Christ than in conceiving the flesh of Christ.... For his brothers, his relatives according to the flesh, who did not believe in him, of what advantage was that relationship? Even her maternal relationship would have done Mary no good unless she had borne Christ more happily in her heart than in her flesh.[32]

Mary lived exactly what Augustine observed. She not only received Christ from her womb, but Mary also received him as Lord and Savior and made herself one of his true followers.

I'm convinced Mary understood precisely what Jesus was asking of her in that backroom wedding conversation. She understood the obstacle and, by faith, how to overcome it. Jesus was not there to affirm her or work all his powers for her interests. Mary understood Jesus's lesson. She responded to Jesus in an equally unexpected way.

It would have been easy to have taken Jesus's words as a rebuke. It would have been easier to shrink away or to have interpreted his words as a moody and definitive no. Was Jesus not rejecting her request? Maybe it was none of their business? But Mary recognized more in Christ's response. Jesus was not objecting to the need; he was objecting to any relational expectation that might keep her from receiving him as Lord. Jesus asked a question of discipleship. Mary responded in the true language of a disciple.

Having absorbed Jesus's words of distance and offense, Mary turned to the nearby servants and commanded them, "Do whatever he tells you."[33] Jesus was Lord. She would submit to his command. And that day, Jesus performed his first miracle. He turned water into wine, saved the party, and began the clock counting down to his final hour. He stepped into the groom's role and gave to those in need. The family was praised for having saved the best wine until last, but it was Jesus who had given it. It was Jesus who secretly gave for the sake of others. And he would do the same again and again. He would do it when the wine was his own blood.

Commentator Rodney Whitacre writes, "Here is a free, full, extravagant outpouring, and it is precisely the Son of God's gratuitous, gracious generosity that is the glory revealed in this sign."[34] Jesus's first sign, so critical to John's gospel, is an act of abundant generosity that rescues a family from their failures and restores the celebration of marriage. But for Mary, it was also a clear reminder of who he really was and what that meant for her.

We've observed in the last chapters many of Jesus's most difficult sayings. He has called for us to die to ourselves, reject division, abandon possessions, and hate family, but a pattern has also emerged. Christ never asks for anything which he does not return in even greater proportion. It has been true of each of his difficult sayings. To the disciple willing to die to self, Jesus promised salvation. To those willing to set down the group identity and come to him as an individual, Jesus offered a new identity. To those willing to renounce their achievements and possessions on earth, Christ promised the treasure of heaven. It is also true of our relationships.

When we learn to die to our expectation of earthly relationships, Christ gives us a new means for even greater relationships. When we hate father, mother, brother, sister, and even ourselves, we are given a new love that frees us to love others in ways we previously could not. We are freed to love one another, to love spouses as Christ loved the church, and to love enemies by turning the other cheek. We are freed from the desperate need to be loved and set free to love neighbors as ourselves and to welcome believers as our own brothers and sisters. When we give up searching for affirmation in earthly relationships, we are given an eternal relationship capable of actually freeing us from insecurity.

As C. S. Lewis so eloquently observed, "Nothing that you have not given away will be really yours. Nothing in you that has not died will ever be raised from the dead. Look for yourself, and you will find in the long run only hatred, loneliness, despair, rage, ruin, and decay. But look for Christ and you will find Him, and with Him everything else thrown in."[35]

We must be willing to ask hard questions about our need for affirmation and how it is polluting not only our earthly relationships but also our relationship with God. Where are we demanding too much? Where are our expectations too high? To whom have we given our trust? What word are we refusing to hear?

The true disciple wants only the truth, even when it comes as a hard word. For it is the truth alone that sets us free. Truth does what no cheap word of affirmation can. Christ, above all others, has come to offer you the truth: the truth of this world, his kingdom, and of yourself.

* * *

"So Jesus said to the Jews who had believed him, 'If you abide in my word, you are truly my disciples, and you will know the truth, and the truth will set you free.'" — John 8:31–32

ACCUSATION: "TOSS IT TO THE DOGS"

"'It is not right to take the children's bread and throw it to the dogs.'
She said, 'Yes, Lord, yet even the dogs eat the crumbs that fall from
their masters' table.'"

MATTHEW 15:26-27

"Anything that disappears from your psychological inventory is apt to turn
up in the guise of a hostile neighbour, who will inevitably arouse your anger
and make you aggressive. It is surely better to know that your worst enemy
is right there in your own heart."

CARL JUNG[1]

Jesus was tired. His ministry around Galilee was drawing larger crowds and the attention of leaders from Jerusalem. The controversy was building. Political and religious rulers always worry when the crowds are not their own. The success of Jesus's movement in Galilee was raising concerns in Jerusalem, which quickly turned into objections. Jesus withdrew to the land of Tyre and Sidon, a gentile region and an unlikely place for a Jewish teacher to spend time. But that's what Jesus was looking for, somewhere he wouldn't be found. He and his disciples needed time to rest.

Their rest was short-lived. A local gentile woman somehow discovered Jesus's location and came with a request. A demon plagued her daughter, and the mother relentlessly called out for Jesus's help. The disciples were irritated. This was exactly what they had been hoping to avoid. They asked Jesus for permission to excuse the woman and send her away. But Jesus was strangely silent. The woman continued to cry out for help. The disciples continued to grow frustrated. Jesus did not speak.

The Pharisees' charges must have been on the disciples' minds as they attempted to rid themselves of that bothersome and unclean gentile woman. People like her were costing Jesus credibility in Jerusalem. Matthew's gospel specifically labeled her a Canaanite. Matthew chose to identify her with her ancestors, which super-charged the moment's tension. The Canaanites had long been Israel's enemy in battle and in worship. The Canaanites had tempted many Israelites into pagan worship. Scholar Craig Blomberg explains, "No one in the first century used that term anymore; Matthew is deliberately conjuring up distasteful memories of the pagan Tyrians and Sidonians from OT times."[2] To label her a Canaanite is a kind of accusation, just the thing the disciples were feeling.

Surprisingly, the woman did not approach as an enemy. Instead, she called out to Jesus as "Lord, Son of David."[3] The title again settled the scene into the old boundary lines of Israel's identity. But even as she identified Jesus as the true king of Israel, Jesus still remained silent. She continued to ask for help; the disciples continued to ask permission to remove her. Finally, Jesus spoke, but he did not answer either her request or the disciples' concerns. "I was sent only to the lost sheep of the house of Israel," he explained. The disciples must have taken it as clear permission to dismiss her, but the woman renewed her effort. "Lord, help me!" she cried out. [4]

Jesus spoke again. "It is not right to take the children's bread and throw it to the dogs."[5] It is a surprising thing to hear Jesus say. It certainly risked offense. Many readers continue to find it offensive. That Jesus would call a gentile woman a dog seems strangely out of character and is certainly offensive to modern readers. So much so that some commentators have speculated that the saying is corrupt and has been edited by later Jewish Christians who meant every possible accusation that pejorative implied. Unable to reconcile such a hard word from our Savior's mouth, these commentators blame the prejudice of those Christians who later added to the story.

But such theories miss how Jesus routinely risked offense. Having learned to recognize how Jesus used the potential of offense, we recognize the deeper truth Jesus was attempting to expose through his words. It was, in the end, that very thing the woman also recognized, for she was not offended by his saying. Instead, she answered, "Yes, Lord, yet even the dogs eat the crumbs that fall from their masters' table."[6] For her ability to overcome the obstacle of his offense, Jesus credited her with great faith.

* * *

If you smooth out the offense of Jesus's statement to diminish it, you also end up diminishing the remarkable faith the woman showed and Jesus's broader point about the accusations that plague the world. To see it you must also recognize that faith and offense are deeply connected. Key to understanding what made her faith great is understanding how the moment's potential for offense was also great. To call someone a dog was as offensive in the ancient world as much as is today. It might even have been more offensive.

Scripture often refers to dogs and always negatively. Though families may have kept dogs for work purposes, they were not considered members of the family as many canine pets are today. In Scripture, dogs were unclean scavengers and predators. Proverbs depicts the dog lapping up its own vomit. Goliath ridiculed David for coming against him with a staff. "Am I a dog?" Goliath mocked. In 2 Kings, the dogs devour the corpse of Jezebel, pushed from a balcony window. Luke describes the dogs licking a poor man's diseased sores. In Philippians, the label dog is used to describe evildoers, and in Revelation, it is used for those who will be rejected from the new heaven and earth, including practitioners of magic arts, the sexually immoral, and murderers. Everywhere, the dog is an unclean image of scorn.[7]

Depicting the Canaanite woman as a dog aligned with the old Jewish tradition of associating the Canaanites with unclean pagan idol worship. She might have been offended, but Jesus's disciples would have found it a fitting image. She was not one of the children of Israel. She was unclean and, like a dog, had come to Jesus scavenging for her own needs. They might even have applauded Jesus's clever image, especially having already made up their minds to dismiss her. She represented everything they sought to distance themselves from. The disciples were concerned with offending important religious leaders, not random gentile women. They took their insecurities out on that woman. They leveled all their resentment, blame, and frustration on her presence.

The disciples were caught up in an escalating feud of accusations, and Jesus risked offending all of them to make them see it. He did so to expose and break the power of accusation, for such spirits of accusation are always the final outcome of insecurity. Jesus would force them to see the real source of their accusations.

When Pharisees from Jerusalem confronted Jesus about his associations and lack of ritual purity, Jesus responded with equally charged language. He explained that it wasn't what a person put into their body that made them unclean, but rather what came out of a person's heart. The Pharisees were careful about appearing to be clean, but their hearts were not clean. Jesus quoted Isaiah to them. "This people honors me with their lips, but their heart is far from me."[8] They were blind to their own hearts and Jesus labeled them hypocrites.

These were important religious leaders to be respected by any serious Jew. Who was Jesus to speak to them with such disrespect? Jesus was from Nazareth and taught in the region of Galilee. The Pharisees he addressed were among the most elite teachers in all of Israel. They held prominent positions of authority and respect in Jerusalem. Jesus's disciples were shocked by how Jesus had treated them. As the Pharisees left, the disciples confronted Jesus and asked, "Do you know that the Pharisees were offended when they heard this saying?"[9]

The Pharisees weren't the only ones fixed on outward appearance. Jesus's own disciples found themselves blinded by the luster of elites. The Pharisees looked down on the disciples for not following their traditions. The disciples were worried about offending reputable and influential people like the Pharisees. They all talked about cleanliness, but really they were paying attention to their positions and respectability. They wielded accusation as much from their own insecurity as from faith. What mattered to them was respect and the acquisition of influence. The disciples showed themselves to be more in mind with the Pharisees than Jesus.

Jesus offered them a parable. "Every plant that my heavenly Father has not planted will be rooted up." Peter asked for an explanation. They didn't understand the parable. "Are you also still without understanding?"[10] Jesus asked. Jesus had used that parable before. And he had explained it before. Jesus loved the image of the gospel as a seed. The sower cast seed into the soil of our hearts. If the soil was good, it would grow. But there were many things that could obstruct and destroy its growth.

When Jesus had previously explained the Parable of the Sower, he had listed several ways the gospel could be thwarted. The second was the rocky ground of persecution and rejection. The seed grows until suffering comes, until rejection begins. Under the pressure of accusation, the seed is spoiled. Jesus explained that the person "immediately falls away." [11] But Jesus meant more than a casual indifference. Jesus used the word *scandalizō*. The KJV translates it, "by and by he is offended." When accusation from the world comes, suddenly, a person is offended by Jesus and his gospel. Salvation sounds good until it costs us respectability, until it means rejection from the world's influential people. Then we encounter an obstacle and find the good news suddenly an offense.

Jesus's encounter with the Canaanite woman followed immediately after Jesus's confrontation with the Pharisees and the concerns of his disciples. I think Jesus saw in that woman an opportunity to illustrate the parable his disciples struggled to understand. They wanted to flatter the Pharisees and earn their respect. They wilted under the pressure of accusation. They imagined the good news spread through influence and reputation. Were they not more interested in affirmation? But Jesus offended them. He offended the Canaanite woman, too. Jesus risked offending the Pharisees, his own disciples, and the Canaanite woman. He let them experience the truth of his parable. He demonstrated that any plant which God had planted, any true faith of the heart, could not be torn up by mere offense. Those of faith would endure the offense of this world, but those without real faith would stumble over it. Jesus tugged on each plant and exposed where the gospel had really taken root.

To the disciples, the Canaanite woman was a weed. She was not a child of Israel but an unclean dog. They felt no need to impress her or show her respect. So, they became the accusers just as they had been accused. They imitated the very accusation the Pharisees had against them. But the woman persisted where the Pharisees could not. She overcame offense and accusation. She would not go away. She would have Jesus or nothing. She demonstrated the mark of true faith.

Imitation that forms in our insecurity and idolatry has a deadly side effect: rivalry. Beneath our consciousness, the same models that inspire our desires also begin to inspire our contempt. Imagining our desires to be authentically our own, we are blind to the forces of competition and conflict forming between us. The more we desire, the more we envy, the more suspicion festers, and blame becomes our excuse. We turn on one another, pointing a finger of accusation at anyone blocking our way or refusing us the affirmation we crave.

IMITATION ALWAYS PRODUCES ACCUSATION

In 2014, researchers at the University of Haifa in Jerusalem investigated the source of rivalry and the resulting joy we often feel at a rival's misfortune.[12] In their experiment, a mother and her child, sometimes as young as twenty-four months, were placed in a test room with an unrelated child of the same age. The two children were encouraged to play as the mother read a book out loud to herself. A cue was given for the mother to pick up a nearby glass of water and intentionally spill it on her book, acting as if it had been an accident. The researchers secretly observed the children's reactions to her misfortune and noted some children showed no interest at all.

Next, the researchers changed the scenario to create what they called an unequal condition for the two children. In the second test, the mother was instructed to place the non-related child on her lap. She was told to praise the child while reading the book specifically to them. It doesn't take much for a small child to become envious of another child receiving their parent's attention. The researchers created this envy as a way of forming a rivalry between the two children. One received affirmation while the other did not.

Again, on cue, the mother intentionally spilled her water on her book. The researchers observed the children's responses. This time, the child who had been provoked to rivalry was far more likely to express pleasure at their mother's misfortune, with some of the test children jumping up and down in excitement and some even verbalizing their satisfaction at her failure. The final research paper explained, "The water spill manipulation was used to provoke schadenfreude as this emotion is frequently provoked following a misfortunate termination of a competitive situation."[13] The researchers finally suggested that individuals with low self-esteem—that is, insecurity—are prone to greater envy and an increase of schadenfreude.

You might not be familiar with the term *schadenfreude*, but you certainly have experienced it. It's why those internet fail videos are so satisfying and addictive. It's why we find deep gratification at news of a rival sport team's loss or the embarrassing gaffe of a politician from an opposing party. The answer is schadenfreude, a German word for the pleasure we feel at another's misfortune, and it is deeply connected to the rivalries that emerge from mimetic desire. Wherever our desires begin to form around a model, rivalry and conflict are likely to form as well.

Your local supermarket magazine stand is a good place to observe how imitation and rivalry are related. Magazine covers on most newsstands can be grouped into two types: celebrity achievements and celebrity failures. Side by side, you're likely to find highly photoshopped, complimentary photos of celebrities and often those same people caught in humiliating and embarrassing tabloid photos. We love seeing them at their best and their worst. Their potential inspires us, and their failures help us feel better about ourselves. It's not just celebrities though. Researchers have found that, though we often deny it, most of us feel real pleasure at the failure of a competitive coworker or family member as well.

Just as our imitation of others is hard to acknowledge, so too are the competitions that form along with them. There is something we secretly desire in our rival, something which inspires our desire and simultaneously moves us into competition with them. The researchers who identified this emotion in children as young as two concluded, "A misfortune befalling on someone we are jealous of reverses the unfavorable comparison and may have an ameliorating effect on self-esteem."[14] For all our culture's talk about improving self-esteem and believing in ourselves, it turns out one of our most effective methods for doing so is seeing a rival's humiliation. We live in a zero-sum world: for us to feel good about ourselves, we need others to feel bad.

From Hollywood's most famous actors to the coworker on the other side of your cubicle wall, and even that viral video of the skateboarder crashing on the rail, your desires are shaped by them, and your self-esteem is shaped by their failures as much as it is your own achievements. You may not have achieved your deepest desires, but you likely feel better about that when seeing your rival fail too.

This common feeling of schadenfreude exposes just how much our identities are formed by both imitation and accusation.

René Girard recognized that the consequence of imitation is inevitably rivalry. While we may imagine ourselves to be original, we both model ourselves on what we observe in others and, through careful and constant comparisons, hope that those models fail. In the twisted logic of our subconscious insecurity, their failure feels like our gain. We want to win—or at least for them to lose. Girard observed,

> When scandals proliferate, human beings become so obsessed with their rivals that they lose sight of the objects for which they compete and begin to focus angrily on one another. As the borrowing of the model's object shifts to the borrowing of the rival's hatred, acquisitive mimesis turns into a mimesis of antagonists.[15]

Girard observed that our desire produces competition that turns our attention away from the object of common desire and instead onto the person keeping us from obtaining it. Failing to secure the affirmation we crave, we begin to imitate the conflict as well as the desire. We begin to obsess over the obstacles in our way. What was once a desire and even a hidden admiration can turn into resentment. As our desires fail to deliver, we look for someone to blame.

The Bible is full of examples of this mimetic rivalry. Consider the archetypal first brothers, Cain and Abel. The competition that arose over the rejection of Cain's sacrifice turned to comparison, rivalry, and eventually to murder. What had Abel done but be accepted where Cain was not? Or consider another pair of brothers,

Jacob and Esau. Their growing rivalry and shared desire led Jacob to impersonate and steal from his brother, later fleeing under the threat of escalating violence. There were also the rivalries of David and Saul, Sara and Hagar, Rachel and Leah, Joseph and his brothers. The Bible is full of these competitive rivalries, each casting blame and accusation, each focused on an object—a crown, a blessing, a child—that soon gave way to envy, jealousy, and offense.

Girard called these points of conflict scandals. And it's not hard to recognize how they bring about the experience of offense. Remember that the Jewish concept of offense is visualized by a blind traveler stumbling over an obstacle. These mimetic rivalries quickly become obstacles in our path. There must be someone to blame. We begin to imagine that our rivals are keeping us from our desires. They, like that obstacle in our path, prevent us from making progress. We become increasingly convinced that they are to blame for our failures and increasingly self-justified in our rivalry with them. We find ourselves more sensitive to being offended by them as well. We become hyper-focused on comparison and sensitive to even the smallest slights. Everything slides into accusation.

The Russian novelist Fyodor Dostoevsky understood how powerful and petty these rivalries can be and how they usually surface as feelings of offense. In his novel *Notes from Underground*, Dostoevsky described a man desperately insecure and resigned to living in the margins of life. Isolated, lonely, and disillusioned, the underground man didn't experience his insecurity as subservience; instead, he raged with resentment and endless comparisons. The more insecure he felt, the more his pride swelled and the more he found people to blame. Dostoevsky's novel is profound partly for its strangeness. His character's obsessions appear ridiculously small and insignificant, but Dostoevsky used them to help us recognize our own strange obsessions and pettiness.

In one scene, the underground man stands in a billiard room watching others play pool. He doesn't realize he's blocking the doorway until a large, six-foot Russian police officer, without speaking a word, picks him up and physically moves him out of the way. The underground man is immediately offended. He wishes the officer would have argued with him, even fought him. What bothers him most is how the officer simply dismissed him. He wrote, "I could not forgive his having moved me without noticing me."[16]

As the days pass, the man becomes obsessed with the incident and with the officer. The insult grows in his mind, and he imagines challenging the officer to a duel. He plots revenge, though these plots also seem small and petty. He determines that the next time they meet on the street, he'll refuse to move and he'll force the officer to alter his path. He plays the scene over and over in his mind. The rivalry festers always beneath the surface.

Though he constantly speaks of the officer as his rival, there is also a strange passage in which he imagines how the two of them might have been friends. He imagines how, with his intellect and the officer's strength, they could have been fused together into a kind of unstoppable force. In another strange detail, he also becomes obsessed with finding enough money to buy a fur coat, one which might give him the appearance of being of a higher class and earning the officer's recognition and acknowledgment. It's not hard to recognize both the accusations and the craving for affirmation.

Though the underground man never admits it, he both despises the officer and deeply admires him. He was both offended and obsessed because he wanted what the officer possessed: respect, recognition, and an appearance of importance. The most impassioned cries of accusation often create a kind of deranged obsession. Increasingly, the underground man valued and even pursued what the officer represented, the very thing he claimed to be most offended by. In his accusation, he became came like him. There is an awkward form of imitation that begins to emerge, and, as it does, it further deepens the conflict and rivalry. You can see how the officer becomes an obstacle upon which the underground man continues to trip and yet continues to return.

This rivalry may seem absurdly small to you, but recognize that to him, it felt all-consuming. Something kept him from letting go. It took on a moral significance. His identity and sense of meaning were both caught up in it. You do it too. You play the game and feel the emotions. The question is, do you recognize the source of your own rivalries? In another of his novels, Dostoevsky explained:

> A man who lies to himself is the first to take offense. It sometimes feels very good to take offense, doesn't it? And surely he knows that no one has offended him, and that he himself has invented the offense and told lies just for the beauty of it, that he has exaggerated for the sake of effect, that he has picked on a word and made a mountain out of a pea—he knows all that, and still he is the first to take offense, he likes feeling offended, it gives him great pleasure, and thus he reaches the point of real hostility.[17]

What Dostoevsky recognized was that offense is a symptom of a much deeper work. Where there is offense, there is always a complex machine turning in the heart. There is always insecurity. There is always envy. And there will always come conflict.

YOUR GREATEST OBSTACLE IS WITHIN

Hearing God approaching, Adam and Eve hid. Whatever the fruit had done, it had not made them God's equal. They certainly did not feel like gods. Instead, they hid in fear. God asked the question they wanted most to avoid: "Did you eat from the tree that I commanded you not to eat from?"[18]

Adam did not directly answer the question. Instead, while glancing at Eve I imagine, he answered, "The woman whom you gave to be with me, she gave me fruit of the tree, and I ate."[19] Adam, our forefather in sin and casting blame, found a way in that single sentence to blame both his wife and God for his disobedience. Eve had the same impulse. "The serpent deceived me,"[20] she added. In those two sentences, every layer of creation had now been polluted with rivalry: man and woman, humanity and creation, humanity and God.

If the recognition of insecurity and nakedness was the first consequence of sin, then the second was the desire to shift the weight of blame. Insecurity can never recognize its own faults. Instead, we find some way to excuse ourselves. What is the alternative? Admit we're the problem? That seems to only risk acknowledging the insecurity was right all along.

The more we ignore our insecurity and the sources of our desire, the more prone we are to blame others for our failures. Blame becomes our first impulse and our tool of self-justification. Our culture is awash with it. Every news story, every bit of social commentary, every conversation is laced with accusations and criticism of anyone but ourselves. Our expertise in what is wrong with the world is often a strategy for avoiding what is wrong with ourselves. Nothing draws the attention away from ourselves quicker than a finger pointed at another. Jesus warned that it is the speck of dust we notice in another's eye that keeps us from seeing the log in our own.[21]

Held for eight years in a communist Russian work camp, Aleksandr Solzhenitsyn understood this truth of evil. He also articulated it both in his writing and with his own life. Surely, there would be no easier time to blame one's opponent than in being unjustly imprisoned and tortured. But Solzhenitsyn recognized that evil cannot be neatly cast onto the other, no matter how cruel one's opponent might be. In *The Gulag Archipelago*, Solzhenitsyn wrote, "If only it were all so simple! If only there were evil people somewhere insidiously committing evil deeds, and it were necessary only to separate them from the rest of us and destroy them. But the line dividing good and evil cuts through the heart of every human being. And who is willing to destroy a piece of his own heart?"[22]

Jesus made a similar point by kneeling before the temple and drawing in the dirt with his finger, the adulterous woman they sought to stone cast at his feet. Strangely, though she had been caught in the act of adultery, the Jewish leaders brought her alone to Jesus. They sought his permission to have her executed. Jesus understood that their real motives were far more complicated. They do not seem to have been wrong about her sin, but Jesus recognized that for all their zeal, they had very little attention for their own sin.

They were fixated on her sin as a way to trap Jesus, who was quickly becoming their obsessive rival. They were willing to use the woman as a tool in their conflict with him. They cast blame to obscure their growing insecurity and rivalry with Jesus's ministry.

Jesus gave a simple command: "All right, but let the one who has never sinned throw the first stone."[23] Kneeling, Jesus also began to write with his finger in the dirt. Steeped in the Old Testament Scriptures, the Pharisees and scribes would have recognized Jesus's words and actions as an allusion to Jeremiah. The prophet Jeremiah had written about the sins of Israel being written on their hearts and added, "O Lord, the hope of Israel, all who forsake you shall be put to shame; those who turn away from you shall be written in the earth."[24] Jeremiah and Jesus, by his answer and action, were reminding them that no one got away with anything. Every heart, along with all sin, would one day be exposed. Every sin and motive would be written out. What may be written only in the secrecy of their own hearts would one day also be written on the ground for all to see.

A remarkable thing occurred, and John gives us a particularly meaningful detail. One by one, the accusers put down their stones and walked away. John includes that the first to lay down their stones were the oldest. It's as if they realized with age and experience, there is an accumulation of one's own guilt which cannot be denied. While the story is meant to illustrate the universality of sin, it points even more strongly to the depths to which we'll go to ignore our own, usually by finding another on which to fixate instead. No one thinks of their own hidden sin when fixated on the exposed sins of a person at their feet. The prophet Jeremiah makes it clear, "The heart is deceitful above all things, and desperately sick; who can understand it? 'I the Lord search the heart and test the mind, to give every man according to his ways.'"[25]

Thus the Pharisees weren't the only ones Jesus turned inward in order to recognize their own sin. How easy it would have been for this woman to have cried victim, to have identified herself as justified by the injustice of their ulterior motives. They had used her. But Jesus confronted her too. For that woman, caught in their legalistic schemes, was also given a command. She was also warned by Jesus, "Go, and sin no more."[26]

Initially, she could have concluded that Jesus had taken her side.

How she must have been tempted by a surging sense of her own superiority after witnessing the Pharisees' humiliation. How easily she could have picked up their failure as her own sense of self-justification. But even after recognizing the way in which she had been unjustly used in the Pharisees' schemes, Jesus still commanded her to go and sin no more as well. She too carried sin and now also a temptation to imagine her rival's humiliation as her own salvation. But that is not how salvation works. Jesus took that stone out of her hand just as he had the Pharisees.

It is as easy for a sense of victimhood to blind us to our own needs as it was for the Pharisee's self-righteousness to blind them from their needs. Writing on this temptation of victimhood, Girard recognized an additional tendency in our modern competitions. He explained, "The concern for victims has become a paradoxical competition of mimetic rivalries, of opponents continually trying to outbid one another." He wisely added, "The victims most interesting to us are always those who allow us to condemn our neighbors. And our neighbors do the same. They always think first about victims for whom they hold us responsible."[27]

What Girard observed is that we can be drawn into concern for victims as a kind of accusation meant to soothe our own insecurities. We're all too willing to take up the cause of a victim who happens to give us ammunition against an existing rival, and we always imagine that our rivals produce far more victims than we do. We may talk endlessly about the cause of victims, but we are often motivated to use them as a competition for our own self-promotion.

Girard saw in this new competitive victim culture a distortion of Christianity. He wrote, "Our concern for victims is the secular mask of Christian love."[28] Where Christianity recognized that each person plays the role of both victim and victimizer, today's culture has formed a rivalry around claims of exclusive victimhood. We are quick to imagine ourselves as victims or to imagine we speak for them, but we seem incapable of recognizing that we are all victimizers as well.

Quoting from Isaiah, the apostle Paul, a firsthand witness to the oppression of Rome and to his own history of persecuting God's people, refused to divide the world into victims and victimizers. Instead, he recognized that all of humanity participates in the escalating conflicts of rivalry. Paul wrote, "Their feet are swift to shed blood; in their paths are ruin and misery, and the way of peace they have not known."[29] Paul was not describing oppressors or those who possessed oppressive power; he was describing every human heart. As he concluded, "None is righteous, no, not one."[30] We're happy to use power if we have it. We're just as happy to use the label of victim if it's all we've got.

Far from reducing victimization, our cultural obsession with measuring victimhood has only created expanding categories of grievance that have exploded the world into constantly new debates, new competitions, and endless forms of rivalry. At the root of these conflicts is a practice more dangerous and pervasive than most can imagine. We have unleashed upon ourselves the spirit of accusation.

THE SPIRIT OF ACCUSATION

Scripture tells us that Satan's characteristic tactic is accusation. The name Satan means the one who accuses. He is a liar and a thief, but above all, Satan is an accuser. First given the name in the book of Job, perhaps the oldest book of the Bible, Satan is depicted by his accusing of Job before God. "Job only worships you because things go well for him,"[31] Satan challenged. Using Job's wife, Satan also played his part in the temptation for Job to accuse God in return. "Job, look at what God has taken from you. Curse God and die."[32] It is the same strategy Satan has played since the beginning. He stands between us, throwing accusations in every direction, stirring us into conflict, and blinding us to our real needs. The spirit of accusation that has overwhelmed our modern society has its roots in the schemes and tactics of Satan himself. He will always give us another to blame and obsess over.

Working our insecurities, desires, and disappointments into a crescendo of conflict and accusation, Satan uses his tools to keep us blind and obsessively stumbling over the offense of another. It is how Satan always works and continues to work today. Satan poisons our ability to receive from God by whispering his accusations of blame. "Someone is keeping you from it." "Someone is getting what you deserve." "Someone is blocking your progress." "Your problem is out there; it's them."

Again, Girard makes this satanic connection clear:

> The road on which Satan starts us is broad and easy. ... But then suddenly there appears an unexpected obstacle between us and the object of our desire, and to our consternation, just when we thought we had left Satan far behind us, it is he, or one of his surrogates, who shows up to block the route. This is the first of many transformations of Satan: the seducer of the beginnings is transformed quickly into a forbidding adversary.[33]

The obstacle is a trap. Without Christ exposing it, we have little chance of overcoming its attraction. Insecurity draws us in, and offense is sure to follow.

We never escape the insecurity that set us on our course. We never achieve our goal because an obstacle always stands in our way. It has been, from the beginning, a trap, a lie, a false way. We do not make real progress but only learn the satanic tactic of accusation that turns us against others. This growing obsession further blinds us to our real needs and leaves us increasingly self-obsessed and self-justified in our envy.

The greatest trick of Satan's scheme of accusation is convincing us that what thwarts our progress is external to us. Satan constantly draws our attention away from ourselves and fixates our gaze on some rival. So, he trips us and stalls us from ever making real progress.

In this modern era of innovation and progress, this age of enlightenment and reason, with more wealth and prosperity than any generation before and unprecedented scientific and technological breakthroughs, does it feel like we're actually progressing? Or does it not feel like Babel: the higher we build the more divided and conflicted we become?[34]

We may soon find cures for cancer and even colonize new planets, but we seem no closer to utopia. We're still murdering each other. Still staring with suspicion and envy at our neighbors. Still harboring bitterness and hate. Still smiling secretly at others' falls. Still prone to accuse another before ourselves. We strive after every desire and find an ever-proliferating number of excuses for never arriving. We're still pretty much naked, hiding in bushes, and blaming each other when caught. Satan has taught us well his art of accusation.

Our world is similarly trapped by these external conflicts and divisions, convinced that if we could simply fix our rival, we could solve our own problems. But Christ came to suggest something very different. Christ came that we, like those Pharisees ready to stone the woman caught in adultery, might set down the stone and recognize our own desperate need. We are caught up in it too.

Christ says to you what this world will not. He will even risk offending you to help you see it. Your greatest problem lies within you. It can be solved neither through the world's affirmation nor your reflex to accuse another. If you can't recognize that, be sure that you too are caught up in the tactics and schemes of satanic rivalry and accusation. You are being led and your heart is being stirred by the whispers of a serpent. And it's costing you what Satan works tirelessly to keep you from: the peace and freedom Christ offers instead.

BUT EVEN THE DOGS

It's too simplistic to imagine Jesus only confronting those whom we think need his peace and freedom. For you are one of those who need it. So am I. Instead, what we find is that Jesus offended everyone. He risked offending the Pharisees as they hid their insecurity in accusation. He risked offending his own disciples as they imitated the Pharisees through their own insecurity. And he risked offending a gentile mother desperate to save her daughter. Jesus would not play their game of accusing a rival. He spoke the truth to every person and risked all being offended.

But they were not all offended. That is the remarkable part of the story and perhaps the most important point. That Jesus would say something offensive is not shocking, not for someone who has been carefully reading the Gospels. But that this Canaanite woman would not be offended by what Jesus said is shocking. What it revealed certainly shocked Jesus's disciples.

We have repeatedly observed that Jesus used offense as a tool of revelation. He used offense to give sight to the spiritually blind and to reveal the idols of the heart. He used the conversation with that gentile woman to reveal not only his disciples' distorted imitations but also her faith. Jesus allowed her to reveal her heart and express her genuine faith.

Writing about this passage, author David McCracken concludes, "The Pharisees are offended; the Canaanite woman is not offended. The stark contrast is revelatory, for the opposite of offense is faith, but the only way to faith is through the possibility of offense."[35]

"Yes, Lord," she answered, easily stepping over his obstacle, "but even the dogs eat the crumbs that fall from their master's table." You can't help but be amazed at how clever she was. That clarity is only possible in a disciple who has abandoned self-defense, accusation, and the possibility of being offended. She alone possessed that faith. Jesus answered her, "Woman, you have great faith! Your request is granted." How rare that commendation of faith was. She received an affirmation that the disciples, blind in their desperation, couldn't have imagined.

What made her faith great? She would not stumble over any obstacle of offense. She could endure any word Christ spoke to her. She saw only her need and paid no attention to reputation, status, or accusations which the Pharisees and disciples constantly stumbled over. She became their model. She became their example of faith. She became an offense to their world of mimetic rivalry.

One of the prerequisites to true discipleship is our ability to hear hard things spoken to us. If we stumble hearing Jesus say things we do not want to hear, we cannot follow him. There is no possibility of being his disciple. The disciple must be able to listen without being offended. Pastor Sam Storms explained, "A person of great faith is painfully humble, never taking offense at the truth about himself/herself."[36]

How was this Canaanite woman able to overcome such an offense? She came to Jesus in desperate need. Her daughter was being tormented by the demonic. Any parent facing the helpless feeling of a child's sickness and distress knows immediately how little respectability and petty rivalries matter. What parent, desperate to save their child, is worried about how they appear? Who thinks about their reputation while their child suffers? She knew her need was great. She knew she needed Jesus.

Ultimately, we need the hard words of Jesus precisely because we do not want to hear them. We need them because cheap affirmation will not solve what ails us. We need his hard words because they are the only way to break through the lines of accusation that have trapped us in our trenches of defense. We need Jesus's hard words because they create an opportunity for faith. His hard words allow us to humble ourselves and submit to his lordship. His hard words let us show ourselves as his true disciples. In the end, it's his hard words that free us from the rivalry and accusations of this world. Jesus's hard words begin the process of real healing.

The greatest challenge you face is not the powers of the world or the rivalry of a neighbor or opponent. Your greatest challenge is acknowledging that you are in need and that the path you're on leads only to your destruction. You need Christ, and no offense should keep you from him.

* * *

"I heard a loud voice in heaven, saying, 'Now the salvation and the power and the kingdom of our God and the authority of His Christ have come, for the accuser of our brothers has been thrown down, who accuses them day and night before our God.'" — Revelation 12:10

CHAPTER 8

HEALING:
"YOU WILL BE OFFENDED BY ME"

"Then Jesus said to them, 'You will all fall away because of me this
night. For it is written, 'I will strike the shepherd, and the sheep of
the flock will be scattered.'"

MATTHEW 26:31

"Following Jesus doesn't get us where we want to go. It gets us
to where Jesus goes, where we meet him in Resurrection surprise:
'My Lord and my God!'"

EUGENE PETERSON[1]

In 1857, archaeologists in Rome found what is currently the oldest
known depiction of Jesus and his crucifixion. Believed to have been
carved by a Roman slave on a plaster wall near the Palatine Hill,
somewhere between the first and second century, the image depicts
a man in a posture of worship, one hand raised. He faces a crucified
man on a cross. But the crucified man, arms stretched across the
beam, has the head of a donkey. Beneath the image, Greek letters
inscribe "Alexamenos worships God."

It had long been a Roman tradition to mock Jews as worshipers of a donkey God. For example, the Roman historian Tacitus joked that a wild herd of donkeys led the Hebrews through the wilderness. Both the ancient writers Josephus and Tertullian refuted the association, but it was widespread enough to have become a common association with both Jewish and Christian worshipers.

Christians did not begin using the sign of the cross as a symbol of their worship until probably the fourth century, when the religion became acceptable under the emperor Constantine. The Roman historian Cicero wrote, "The mere name of the cross, should be far removed, not only from the persons of Roman citizens—from their thoughts, and eyes, and ears. For . . . the bare possibility of being exposed to them—the expectation, the mere mention of them even—is unworthy of a Roman citizen and of a free man."[2]

Yet, some Roman, in a spare moment of time, took out his knife and carved on that plaster wall the image of a donkey-headed man crucified and worshiped. Was it meant to mock some Christian who lived there, to tease a friend, or was it carved to put down the spreading ideas of Christianity? It is not, in the end, all that surprising that the oldest known image of Christ and of his crucifixion was not an icon in an ancient church; it was not painted by a converted Christian artist; it was not a symbol of honor or respect at all. Instead, the oldest image of Christ crucified was a piece of crude graffiti meant to mock the worship of Christian believers. It was an image of offense.

To even the slaves of Rome, the cross and the Christ worshiped on it was a joke. Jesus and his crucifixion was an offense. It had long been that way. It still is.

* * *

On the night Jesus was betrayed, he gathered his disciples and began to teach them. He washed their feet. He broke bread and passed them his cup. They ate and sang hymns together. And Jesus warned them. Passing through the dark streets of Jerusalem and up onto the Mount of Olives, Jesus explained, "You will be offended by me this night."[3] He reminded them of the words from the prophet Zechariah, "I will strike the shepherd, and the sheep of the flock will be scattered."[4] Peter objected, "Though they are all offended by you, I will never be offended."[5]

Jesus looked at Peter and went further, "Truly, I tell you, this very night, before the rooster crows, you will deny me three times."[6] Most of us remember the dramatic scene of Peter's denials, but Peter was not alone in abandoning Jesus. All of Jesus's disciples were offended. They stumbled over his arrest, trial, and death. His cross became an obstacle to them, and they scattered. Yet Jesus knew that the real obstacles that awaited them were more than just the next day's suffering.

Jesus knew that his cross would continue to be an offense even after his resurrection, and they would be tempted to deny him again because of it. If they were to follow him, what awaited was their own rejection, persecution, and for many of them, their own executions. As his disciples, they would carry the offense of the cross with them for the rest of their lives.

In John's gospel, Jesus offered a longer warning. He told them,

I have said all these things to you to keep you from falling away. They will put you out of the synagogues. Indeed, the hour is coming when whoever kills you will think he is offering service to God. And they will do these things because they have not known the Father, nor me. But I have said these

169

things to you, that when their hour comes you may remember that I told them to you.[7]

Jesus specifically warned his disciples of their own coming rejection and suffering so that they would not be offended when it came to them too.

Jesus had often spoken of offense and had risked offending them by his words, but on that final night, he turned his attention to the offense they would have to overcome within their own hearts. In those final hours before his death, Jesus urged them not to be offended by what was to come. For a long time, Jesus had been using offense to prepare them for the offense ahead. He had been using offense as a tool to expose their hearts and draw them deeper into discipleship, knowing that they would encounter a greater offense still ahead of them. They would encounter that offense in his rejection and cross and in their own forthcoming rejections and ridicule.

Jesus had been using offense with his disciples to prepare them. When a person receives a vaccination, the goal is to introduce a small, weakened dose of the actual disease. The immune system is given a chance to learn to overcome the threat and allowed to plan for encountering the threat later in its fuller form. The best immunity is provided not through avoidance, but through encountering. Jesus did not protect his disciples by hiding them away. He did not shelter them from offense. Instead, he gave them small doses of offense so they might learn from it. He offended them to open their eyes. He offended them so that they might fix their eyes on him. He risked offending so they would not be offended by the things to come.

So it is with all true disciples. Jesus does not coddle us and risk our being naïve and immature to the temptations of the world. He guides us. Teaches us. Trains us. Even disciplines us. He exposes what is in us and what is in the world.

Jesus's hard words serve to uncover and break the mechanism of offense prone to ensnare you. Hopefully, you are beginning to recognize not only how this mechanism is at work within your own heart but also how Jesus challenges it and frees you from it. Jesus teaches his disciples how to recognize their own insecurity and false desires. He teaches them to recognize their idolatry and imitations. He teaches them to avoid cheap affirmation and to abandon the spirit of accusation, which continues to plunge the world into escalating offense. Jesus let his disciples experience offense so that they might recognize it in all its tempting forms.

Though Jesus's disciples were offended that night, they soon learned the lesson. They soon escaped the trap and would prove it with their lives. Peter would deny Christ—and be forgiven. And as Jesus explained, Peter would go on to face his own rejection and persecution, yet even as Peter was himself crucified, he would not deny Christ again. Peter would preach with boldness to the crowds and give his life willingly to affirm the faith that had finally captured his whole attention. How does that kind of change take place in a person? How do we go from cowardice to that kind of courage? How do we overcome the mechanism of offense, which constantly risks tripping us and entrapping us in envy and rivalry? How do we become like Christ and less like the world?

WHAT ARE YOU IMITATING?

There is much talk today of Jesus bringing salvation, which he does. It is not hard to preach Jesus's forgiveness of sins or his love for the broken and downtrodden. But Jesus does not come merely that we would be forgiven. He came so that we might also see him and learn to follow him. It is true he was the friend of sinners, but he was friend enough to tell them the truth and call them to repentance.

Jesus took on flesh. He dwelt amongst us. The truth of his incarnation is, most profoundly, that the invisible God took on visible form. Why would God come to us in this form of physical, tangible flesh? In seeing Jesus, our eyes are given a new object upon which to fix their gaze. We are given a new model to imitate. Seeing Jesus, fixing our eyes on him, allows us to take our eyes off the things of this world. Jesus came that we might imitate him.

Writing in *Practice in Christianity*, Kierkegaard explained,

> Now, it is of course well known that Christ continually uses the expression "imitators." He never says that he asks for admirers, adoring admirers, adherents; and when he uses the expression "follower" he always explains it in such a way that one perceives that "imitators" is meant by it, that is not adherents of a teaching but imitators of a life.[8]

To follow Jesus is to imitate him. He is not a philosophy, not only a teacher, nor a collection of wise advice. Jesus is a model to be imitated.

Much of this book has been about imitation. To be human is to imitate. It's how we learn, it's how we grow, and as we have seen, it's how our values and desires are formed. As American Philosopher Eric Hoffer concluded, "When people are free to do as they please, they usually imitate each other."[9] We will imitate even into our own death. We imitate even as we are trapped by it. We can't help ourselves and rarely recognize we're doing it. Perhaps, having seen all the challenges associated with imitation, you might conclude that the solution to man's envy and offense is simply to stop imitating others: stop imitating and the whole mechanism of offense is disrupted. But imitation is inescapable.

Everything we know has come from some form of imitation. The Scriptures do not, in the end, encourage us to abandon imitation. What the gospel offers is a new imitation. Jesus introduces the possibility of a new imitation, a new model to fix our eyes upon, and by that imitation, new desires to be discovered. Because, remember, it is always what we imitate that produces what we desire. The Bible calls this discipleship. Jesus not only came to save us, but he also came to call us his disciples. He calls us to imitate him.

When I was young, it used to be an evangelical cliché to ask, "What would Jesus do?" Many of us had the acronym stitched onto bracelets and printed on T-shirts. It is how we thought about being a disciple. We tried to do just what Jesus had done. Act like him, and you'll be like him. The question attempted to reorient our imagination into the motivations and actions of Jesus. But I'm not sure we really understood what we were asking. I seem to remember thinking that I could simply read the Bible and, from the Gospels' stories, implement Jesus's ways of behaving into my modern high school context. But it never worked out that cleanly.

We are faced with innumerable questions that simply didn't exist in the first century. And to imagine that the goal of Christian discipleship is only to correct behavior is to ignore the powerful force of desire driving our behavior. Perhaps today's cultural emphasis on pursuing your own desires is a consequence of having imagined that desire could simply be ignored. To ignore desire in favor of mere action is to miss the real lesson of discipleship. We are made disciples not only to change our actions but also to discover, through the imitation of Jesus, new desires created in us. The offering of Christ is not to follow and ignore your desires. The offering of Christ is to follow and find your desires changed. To really imitate Jesus is to begin desiring new things, what he desires.

Girard explained this form of Christian imitation, writing,

> What is the basis of imitating Jesus? It cannot be his ways of being or his personal habits: imitation is never about that in the Gospels. Neither does Jesus propose an ascetic rule of life in the sense of Thomas à Kempis and his celebrated *Imitation of Christ*, as admirable as that work may be. What Jesus invites us to imitate is his own desire, the spirit that directs him toward the goal on which his intention is fixed: to resemble God the Father as much as possible.[10]

It is only through the imitation of Christ that we are changed to the depths of our real needs and insecurities.

The mark of a real disciple is not only the physical act of following; the real mark of discipleship is the development of new desires in line with Christ. That takes time. It took years for Jesus's first disciples. Even as they watched Jesus crucified, their old desires for self-preservation proved overpowering. But that would change. As Christ breathed on his disciples and as they received his Spirit, they suddenly found their desire to obey and even die for him far more compelling than their old desires for themselves.

That is the mark of a real follower of Jesus. We have discovered new desires in ourselves, having seen those desires lived out in Christ's death and resurrection on our behalf. They are not our own achievements formed through self-discipline and effort, lest we should boast in ourselves. They are desires formed in us by focusing our eyes on Jesus, by looking more closely at what he has done. His cross compels us to take up our own. We begin to desire the same selfless service he has shown us.

Has following Jesus formed those new desires in you? Has following Jesus weakened your imitation of the world? Has it broken the envy and competition and offense you feel? Has following Jesus changed what you want? If you are really living your life as a disciple of Jesus, you should begin to want new things. You should find your desires untangling from the world and reshaping themselves in the form of Christ. If not, perhaps you are not really looking at Christ. Perhaps you are not really imitating him but still imitating the world.

The first disciples did not live in a strict imitation of Jesus's ministry. They did not stay in Galilee or Jerusalem. They did not limit themselves to the Jewish people. They did not even limit themselves to Jesus's teaching. They, after all, had the rest of the story, the full gospel message of what Jesus had not only taught but what he had done. They went out into the world. They were changed by the time they had spent with Jesus.

But they also went with the message of a God who had allowed himself to be crucified by Rome. At first, the disciples, like so many of the Jews around them, rejected the idea of their teacher being arrested and executed. It wasn't until Jesus's resurrection and the pouring out of his Spirit that they began to understand and, more importantly, imitate what Jesus had done. Let me put that more simply: the cross and its offense forced the disciples to receive Jesus finally and to become his disciples fully. For in the cross, our imitation of Jesus is put to its full test. No one wants to imitate the cross. But to be Christ's disciples, that is exactly what we're supposed to do.

Everyone loves the idea of imitating Jesus when it feels pleasant and morally meaningful. Jesus, as a moral teacher of love, offends no one. But few like the idea of imitating Jesus when it means the world's ridicule, isolation, rejection, rebuke, and death. However, you cannot understand Jesus or his true desires without seeing him sacrifice himself. You cannot learn to imitate him while denying any suffering or rejection yourself. Real disciples must inevitably come to the cross. The cross is the real breaking of the worldly trap and the source of all our new God-given desires. As G. K. Chesterton put it, "There is only one thing which is generally safe from plagiarism—self-denial."[11] In dying to our desires, our imitation of the world is broken and our eyes are permitted to see and be changed by Jesus. So it is our willingness to die to ourselves, to take up our own cross, to identify with the crucified servant, which finally breaks the mechanism of offense in this world.

Consequently, it is no real surprise that the cross is where we encounter the world's strongest sensitivity to offense. The world cannot accept the cross because the cross forces us to see our insecurity and need. The cross forces us to recognize that, caught up in the world's imitations, our insecurity is more likely to lead us into participation in his death than allegiance. The cross exposes our denials. The cross exposes our pride. The cross exposes that we are more disciples of the world than Jesus. On the cross, Jesus identified himself with us. And on the cross, he asks us to identify ourselves with him. The cross is insecurity. The cross is the symbol of need. Everything in us rebels against it. We need some path away from it. But the cross calls us into it.

L. Nelson Bell, a missionary, once explained, "When we strip away the unbelievable wordiness of theological controversy today, we find that the burning issue has to do with man's attempt to bypass the offense of the Cross."[12] The cross calls us to die to ourselves and to identify ourselves with him.

THE OFFENSE OF THE CROSS

In Corinth, everyone seemed to be offended. Charges of offense and division consumed their conversations and worship. The church was descending into deeper conflict, stoked by the greed of false teachers and leaders. Christians were constantly accusing and offending one another to prove their own points. They were rallying around celebrities, indulging false desires, and perverting the truth. They were increasingly disinterested in the simple message of the gospel and were perversely enamored with their own power and influence. They showed all the signs of being ensnared by offense. It's easy to see their insecurity, idolatry, imitation, and growing accusations.

Paul, who planted the Corinthian church, faced a real challenge. He wanted to draw them back into unity but knew their aversion to offense divided them. Their unwillingness to embrace the offense of the cross left them sensitive to every other offense. No longer identifying with the offense of the cross, they no longer possessed the humility to be corrected. Before he could deal with the issues dividing the church, he needed to risk offending them.

Paul opened his first letter to the Corinthians by writing, "I, when I came to you, brothers, did not come proclaiming to you the testimony of God with lofty speech or wisdom. For I decided to know nothing among you except Jesus Christ and him crucified."[13] Earlier in the letter, he wrote, "For Jews demand signs and Greeks seek wisdom, but we preach Christ crucified, a stumbling block to Jews and folly to Gentiles."[14] Paul recognized that the fundamental issue in Corinth was their aversion to the cross. The cross was foolish and offensive to them. Ironically, as they rejected the offense of the cross, they became increasingly offended by one another. Paul understood that the offense of the cross was the only way to overcome the offenses of the world.

Paul could have attempted to regain unity by trying to eliminate all offenses. He could have urged them simply to have accepted one another. He could have asked them to accept their differences and embrace one another in the name of love. But it wouldn't have worked. They would have ended up fighting over who was better at love. They needed a force that could change the desires that divided them. We cannot change our behavior without new desires. As C. S. Lewis explained, "I cannot, by direct moral effort, give myself new motives. After the first few steps in the Christian life we realise that everything which really needs to be done in our souls can be done only by God."[15]

We began this book by looking at the underlying insecurity that entered the world through the serpent's temptation in the garden. We saw how that insecurity gave birth to desire, imitation, and conflict. We saw how those underlying mechanisms of offense led to a world of offense. The cross exposed all of it. First, at the cross, our insecurity was put on full display. Remember how the religious leaders were terrified of losing their power and influence. Pilate was afraid of the instability Jesus was causing. Jesus's own disciples became insecure about their association with him. The leaders sought to kill Jesus and the disciples denied him, not out of power but out of insecurity.

We also saw how that insecurity leads us to an imitation of desire. Our imitations fix our eyes on an idol, an object that promises us the power to overcome insecurity. So it was that the death of Christ became their idol, and the crowds began to build in violent imitation. Lines that once divided Sadducees from Pharisees, Romans from Jews, and rich from poor suddenly blurred as they collectively imitated the desire to have Jesus crucified. "It is better for you that one man should die for the people, not that the whole nation should perish,"[16] Caiaphas, the High Priest, reasoned.

Is that not the same mechanisms of offense we observe throughout history and in our own day? The violent mob mentality, the hatred of truth, the silencing of any who oppose. The crowd set against the prophet—humanity in rebellion against the authority of God. At the cross, Jesus became an offense. He became an obstacle that the world united to remove.

Girard notes, "The violent unanimity of the Passion results from a massive transference of scandals, a snowballing so powerful that its effects become inescapable."[17] The cross is the snowballing of offense. It is the exposing of the mechanisms of offense that the world on its own cannot overcome. It is the consequence of a world endlessly insecure and envious. It is the consequences of imitative desire that blinds the heart to its idolatry. On the cross, all of it is put on full display. This is what our hearts naturally produce. We crucify God. Jesus dared offend us, and we determined to kill him for our offense.

The cross forces all of us to choose. We join the crowd in rejecting him, walk away callously indifferent, or we recognize what the cross exposes. We will either be offended or we will be humbled. At the cross, our hearts are either hardened or broken. The cross is the obstacle in our path for which each of us must inevitably reckon.

At the cross, all of humanity faces the potential of offense. The rulers, the religious leaders, the crowd, the disciples. Each was tempted by their own desires. Jesus became an object of the world's distaste. They mocked him. They spit on him. They taunted him and stripped him naked. They humiliated him. They mocked him by calling him king. They wrapped a robe around him, forced a thorny crown on his head, and bowed in mockery. There is no more powerful image of humanity's rejection.

Yet the Bible records that amongst this snowballing of offense, as the crowd's cries built and as the laughing and jeering spread, Jesus was not offended. Jesus was not offended by humanity's most offensive rejection. As Peter later recorded, "When he was reviled, he did not revile in return; when he suffered, he did not threaten, but continued entrusting himself to him who judges justly."[18] Do not imagine that Jesus was not tempted to be offended. In agony, he prayed in the garden, "If it be possible, let this cup pass from me."[19] He knew what awaited him on the cross.

Jesus understood all the temptations of offense and how they would merge at the cross. He knew what it was to have his desires offended, yet he prayed for God's will to be done, not his own. In his suffering, he did not call down the armies of heaven to prove who he was. The God of creation allowed himself to be stripped naked and exposed to the world without a single possession with which to cover himself. He watched his disciples abandon him in his moment of need. He listened as the lowest of society taunted him for their own amusement.

There was no offense he had previously warned his disciples of that he did not have to endure on the cross. There was no offense risked in conversation with others that he himself did not know as well. Yet at each obstacle, he did not stumble. He did not take offense.

Look at him there on the cross. Do you see him in his humiliation? Do you see him for the offense the world has made him? He is silent. He does not defend himself. He does not rebuke those who revile him. He does not curse or argue or protest. Where is his quick wit? Where are his hard words? Where is his word of offense? Where is that sword from his mouth?

On the cross, Jesus does not need to offend by his words. He offends on the cross with his goodness. He offends us by taking our place. He offends us by exposing our sin and our inability to do what he does. He offends now by what he freely gives. Jesus, hanging on the cross, prays, "Father, forgive them, for they know not what they do."[20] But in the cross, we are given a glimpse of exactly what we do.

By his cross, Jesus exposed the world's offense for what it is. We are insecure. We are blind. We are envious. Our eyes look not to God, but to our neighbor in imitative desire. We are quick to divide, to demand, to protect ourselves, and we are caught up in escalating offense. We are offended by God.

Jesus was the only sinless man, and he was the only one capable of enduring this world of offense without succumbing to it. He was without offense. So, he is the only person truly safe to imitate. There is no competition in him. There is no envy or hostility. It is in imitating him that we find our path out of the trap of offense.

The cross is the offense to offense. If you turn from the offense of the cross, you will take up the offenses of this world. It is only by the offense of the cross that you are freed from the offenses of the world. The cross is the singular offense we must not lose, for it frees us from all other offenses. We are called to carry this offense of the cross on our shoulders and to steward in this world. The British writer and preacher John Stott wrote:

> It is there, at the foot of the cross, that we shrink to our true size. And of course men do not like it. They resent the humiliation of seeing themselves as God sees them and as they really are. They prefer their comfortable illusions. So they steer clear of the cross. They construct a Christianity without the cross, which relies for salvation on their works and not on Jesus

Christ's. They do not object to Christianity so long as it is not the faith of Christ crucified. But Christ crucified they detest. And if preachers preach Christ crucified, they are opposed, ridiculed, persecuted. Why? Because of the wounds which they inflict on men's pride.[21]

FREED FROM ALL OFFENSE

In C. S. Lewis's *The Voyage of the Dawn Treader*, Eustace begins as a self-interested brat. Driven by his own greed, Eustace could not leave a hoard of dragon's gold he found. He fell asleep on the treasure, then he woke up and found himself transformed into a dragon. His skin became hardened by thick, dark scales. No one knew of any magic that could reverse it.

If you are familiar with Lewis's Narnia series, you'll also recognize the lion, Aslan, as a type of Jesus. So it was that Aslan appeared to Eustace and commanded Eustace to follow. Afraid of the lion, Eustace obeyed. The lion led the dragon-boy deep into the woods until they came to a garden and a pool of water. Eustace became desperate to get into the water, believing that it would relieve the pain of his scales. But Aslan commanded the boy to remove his scales before he entered the water.

The boy began desperately scratching at his scales. The scales seemed to flake off, but trying to enter the water, Eustace realized his skin was still dark and wrinkled with new scales. Aslan, seeing the child's panic, spoke, "You will have to let me undress you." Lewis records Eustace's memory of it:

> I was afraid of his claws, I can tell you, but I was pretty nearly desperate now. So I just lay flat down on my back to let him do it.

The very first tear he made was so deep that I thought it had gone right into my heart. And when he began pulling the skin off, it hurt worse than anything I've ever felt. The only thing that made me able to bear it was just the pleasure of feeling the stuff peel off. . . .

And there was I as smooth and soft as a peeled switch and smaller than I had been. Then he caught hold of me—I didn't like that much for I was very tender underneath now that I'd no skin on—and threw me into the water. It smarted like anything but only for a moment. After that it became perfectly delicious and as soon as I started swimming and splashing I found that all the pain had gone from my arm. And then I saw why. I'd turned into a boy again.[22]

I wonder if you have known that kind of pain? I wonder if you have felt Christ work that kind of healing in your life?

It is a strange paradox to suggest that we are freed from offense by offense, but it is true. Just as it is true to realize that we have overcome death by death. So, it is only in overcoming the offense of the cross that we are freed from the offense of the world. To overcome the offense of Christ's cross is to find exposed and defeated the offense of your own heart. On the cross, it is all laid bare. It is put to death with Christ.

By rejecting the offense of the cross and rejecting the pain of Christ's healing, we are choosing to wallow in the unending pain and offense of this world. The consequences are all around us. Our society and families are being torn apart. The church is being silenced and transformed. Hate and jealousy pollute the air. We are blind to it, and as it did at the cross, our offense continues to plunge the world into endless imitation of violence and suffering.

But for those who recognize the cross as power to overcome offense, we are freed from it. Oh, we may still suffer the consequences of a world descending into chaos, but that chaos no longer has room in our hearts. Our hearts and their desires have been changed. We now see how it all works. We are still in this world but no longer a part of it. The mechanism has been exposed; our hand removed from the trap. Christ has transformed the obstacle by becoming the obstacle. The stone rejected has been made the cornerstone of a new temple.

"The person who is living by grace sees this vast contrast between his own sins against God and the offenses of others against him," writes author Jerry Bridges. "He forgives others because he himself has been so graciously forgiven. He realizes that, by receiving God's forgiveness through Christ, he has forfeited the right to be offended when others hurt him."[23] By risking offense, Christ actually frees us from it. He extracts the underlying insecurity upon which offense is constructed.

The only hope for our world is Christ and his cross. The only hope of overcoming what offends is recognizing that Christ has done it first. We follow him through the offense to our freedom from it. That is why Kierkegaard called offense, "Christianity's crucial criterion" and the "eternal, essential component of Christianity."[24] You must encounter offense, for the cross sets it before you. To overcome the obstacle of the cross is to be freed from all the offenses of the world. But you must not stumble or be offended by Jesus. You must follow. You must become his disciple. You must allow him to expose your heart and open your eyes. You must decide to repent and imitate him alone.

Peter, having denied Jesus three times, just as Jesus had predicted, found himself again with Jesus on the shores of Galilee.

Who hasn't felt something of his humiliation? He had denied Jesus, and now Jesus stood before him alive and in the full power of his resurrection.

The emotions of that moment are poignant, but there is a simple ambiguity. What did Jesus mean by "more than these?"[25] The word Jesus used was a basic plural pronoun. Do you love me more than these things? Was Jesus referring to the other disciples? Was he referring to the fish fried there by the sea, which had been so fundamental to Peter's way of life? Was Jesus referring to those things that had come before that moment, those things in Peter's history that he must have longed to have undone? Or maybe the ambiguity of Jesus's question was meant to tie together all these things.

We saw early in this book how Peter had received one of Jesus's strongest words of offense. In that rebuke, Jesus had left no ambiguity to Peter's mistake. Peter had taken his mind off Jesus and had been instead focused on the things of man. It had been the things of man, the fear of man, that had led Peter to deny Christ. And so perhaps that day on the shore of the Sea of Galilee, Jesus again pulled Peter away from the things of this world and back to himself. "Do you love me more than these things, Peter?"[26]

Peter's answer was not one of mere religious obedience. He did not answer as if he were attempting to pass some entrance examination. Peter's answer is choked with genuine emotion. Three times, Peter answered Jesus, "Yes, Lord; you know that I love you."[27] What has drawn Peter's attention finally away from the things of the world is not self-discipline, spiritual discipline, or sheer self-determination. What has finally captured Peter's interest, now having fully seen Christ's love for him, is his own love for Christ. After all that they had been through—after all Christ had forgiven—how could Peter ever take offense? Peter had been changed, and the temptations he once stumbled over were now overcome, not by his effort, but by his realization of Christ's goodness and love.

In one of his epistles, Peter seems to be reflecting on this experience:

> As you come to him, a living stone rejected by men but in the sight of God chosen and precious, you yourselves like living stones are being built up as a spiritual house, to be a holy priesthood, to offer spiritual sacrifices acceptable to God through Jesus Christ. For it stands in Scripture:
>
> > "Behold, I am laying in Zion a stone,
> > a cornerstone chosen and precious,
> > and whoever believes in him will not be put to shame."
>
> So the honor is for you who believe, but for those who do not believe,
>
> > "The stone that the builders rejected
> > has become the cornerstone."
>
> and
>
> > "A stone of stumbling,
> > and a rock of offense."[28]

We must not neglect the offense of the cross. We must not turn away from it. We must not ignore it or diminish it. For it is the cross and its offense that hold the power to change us. By the cross, we learn to imitate Jesus. We die with him, but so, too, we are raised to new life with him. Coming upon the cross, we will either stumble over it as an obstacle, or we will recognize that stone in our path as the cornerstone of an entirely new project. By the cross, we are freed from the trap of offense and our imitation of the world.

* * *

"But we preach Christ crucified, a stumbling block to Jews and folly to Gentiles, but to those who are called, both Jews and Greeks, Christ the power of God and the wisdom of God." — 1 Corinthians 1:23–24

CHAPTER 9

SHOULD WE TOO OFFEND?

"However, not to give offense to them, go to the sea and cast a hook and take the first fish that comes up, and when you open its mouth you will find a shekel. Take that and give it to them for me and for yourself."

MATTHEW 17:27

"An honest man speaks the truth, though it may give offense; a vain man, in order that it may."

WILLIAM HAZLITT[1]

Jesus speaks hard truths because, on our own, we are not prone to discovering them. The deepest answers to the most profound questions do not emerge from your own heart or mind. Christ is the answer, and he is also the obstacle that forces you to reckon with who you really are. How can I say something so countercultural without risking offense? How can I speak of the real Jesus at all and not be an offense to this world's projects and self-justifications?

"Act just once in such a manner that your action expresses that you fear God alone and man not at all—you will immediately in some measure cause a scandal," wrote Kierkegaard. "The only thing that manages to dodge scandal is that which out of fear of men and deference to men is completely conformed to the secular mentality."[2] There is, in the end, no faithfulness that can avoid offense. But does that mean we too should seek to offend?

I am not, by nature, a person prone to offending. I don't like it. I take no joy in seeing a person offended. I don't believe Jesus did either. Please do not misunderstand what this book has been about. Jesus did not risk offense simply to provoke offense. He risked offending because it is only by this blow that our eyes are opened to the mechanism of offense in this world. We will either encounter the offense of Christ and overcome it or find ourselves continually plunging deeper into the intensifying offenses of our time.

Is this not the very paradox of the gospel itself? Death has overcome death. And so, too, offense has overcome the offense of the world. The trap of the serpent has been exposed, and we have become wise to his schemes. I hope you have seen it in the world and in yourself. Do not go on ignoring the insecurity you want desperately to deny. See it. Recognize it. See the way that insecurity sets your eyes on the idols of this world. Recognize how those idols create desires and draw you into their imitation. See the way that false self produces greater insecurity. See how it leaves you craving affirmation, which is never fully given. And see the way insecurity produces envy. See the way it pollutes your relationships with accusation and blame. See the way it traps you in greater offense.

There is only one way out. You must allow Jesus to break the trap and set you free. You must turn your eyes to him. You must begin to imitate him and find through him new desires and an end to your deepest insecurities. But the truth is, this is no easy task. Neither is it one which can be finally completed, not in this life. The serpent is always awakening new insecurities and pitching new idols to cure them. And we are constantly tempted to wade deeper into the offense of this world. We are tempted to be offended and to make ourselves the offense. Our own cure is to recognize the game and refuse to play it.

In Luke's gospel, Jesus admitted to his disciples, "It is impossible but that offenses will come."[3] No book can rid the world of it. There is no technique to shelter us from it. You can be sure that you will experience offense. We live in a world full of it, and given the trajectory of our current culture, there will most likely be more of it to come. But Jesus, so often prone to causing offense, also gave his disciples a careful warning. He went on to add about offense, "but woe to the one through whom they come!"[4] Woe to those who cause offense.

LEST WE OFFEND THEM

You should not put down this book thinking that Jesus offended simply to be offensive. You should not think that to be like Jesus you must rush into the world offending to prove the point. You've missed the whole lesson if you imagine Jesus strutting around picking fights simply to offend. If that is how you understand Jesus, then you have yet to really encounter his offense for yourself. Having yet overcome it in your own heart, you are ill-prepared to steward it in the world. So, let me offer you a final conversation in which Jesus said something surprising about his own offense.

Arriving in Capernaum with Jesus, Peter was approached by a local tax collector. The collector noted that Jesus had yet to pay his temple tax. "Does your teacher not pay the tax?"[5] the man asked Peter. He was referring to an annual tax that men over the age of twenty were expected to pay. The tax funded temple sacrifices offered for the nation of Israel. The tax was not required by scriptural law, and some seem to have refused participation. Of course, the temple priests had exempted themselves from paying it, and this tax collector seemed to suggest that Jesus might also have had some conscientious objection.

Peter was quick to affirm Jesus's willingness to pay the tax. It leads you to again wonder about Peter's ongoing concerns for Jesus's reputation. Peter seemed reluctant to risk offending a common social expectation. Promising the payment, Peter went to find Jesus. But Jesus seemed to have sensed Peter's question before he had a chance to ask. Walking into the house, Jesus spoke to Peter first. "From whom do kings of the earth take toll or tax? From their sons or from others?"[6]

It appears to be another classic passage of Jesus's offense. Again, Jesus opposed a tradition being forced on him and his followers. Jesus was being asked to pay a tax from which he recognized he should be exempt. "Does the son have to pay a tax for his father's house?"[7] Jesus asked. The obvious answer was no, which put Jesus at odds with what Peter had told the tax collector. Jesus was willing to turn over tables to protect the integrity of his father's house. This would be another opportunity for Jesus to make the point. Get ready for the offense, we assume.

And, of course, it was again Peter caught in the middle of the tension. It was Peter who had already spoken for Jesus and got it wrong. This story occurs in Matthew's gospel just a few verses after Peter had been rebuked and called Satan. Peter recognized his mistake, answering Jesus's question, "From others." Peter acknowledged that Jesus was not under any obligation to comply. "The sons are free,"[8] Jesus confirmed. But what Jesus said next came as a complete surprise, for it broke his ongoing pattern of offense.

Jesus then said to Peter, "However, not to give offense to them, go to the sea and cast a hook and take the first fish that comes up, and when you open its mouth you will find a shekel. Take that and give it to them for me and for yourself."[9] Is this the same Jesus? Is he reluctant to offend? How is he now so concerned with not offending? The scholar N. T. Wright called this story "one of the most peculiar little stories in the whole New Testament."[10] Not sure what to make of it, many focus on the miraculous provision of a coin from a fish's mouth. But that is not the story's center. The actual description of finding the coin and paying the tax is not even recorded. The story is about Jesus's intentional avoidance of offense.

Jesus had often been willing to risk offense—we've seen plenty of that—but it had always been for the sake of revealing a person's heart. Jesus recognized that the tax collector's request for payment was not a question of his personal desires or even his opinion of Jesus's identity. The man was simply doing the job assigned to him. Jesus had a right to deny payment, but what was to be gained by it? Jesus had not come to defend his own rights. He was not willing to offend to make that point. Jesus understood that offense must be stewarded. He understood that the wrong offense could become an obstacle to encountering the essential offense. There were times offense was to be risked, and times it was not. To risk offense for the sake of his own rights was not its proper use.

It's no coincidence that Matthew next recorded Jesus's specific warning about the danger of offense immediately following this story of the fish and coin. Jesus warned his disciples that anyone who caused a child to stumble would face grave consequences. It was better to be drowned with a millstone around your neck. Though many translations warn of sin and temptation, Jesus specifically used the language of offense. To translate the warning broadly as sin is to miss the thematic point Jesus was making. Jesus was not just warning about sin; he was warning his disciples about placing obstacles in the path of a child's pursuit of God. He was warning his disciples about how to steward offense. Certainly, those obstacles could be sin, but they were to be careful not to give any offense that might hinder a child from following him.

Jesus then warned the disciples that they must also be careful not to let their own bodies lead them into offense. The King James Version preserves the language of offense. Jesus explained, "Wherefore if thy hand or thy foot offend thee, cut them off, and cast them from thee: it is better for thee to enter into life halt or maimed, rather than having two hands or two feet to be cast into everlasting fire."[11] The apostle Paul picked up on this same theme, warning Christians in Corinth and Rome about causing fellow believers to turn away because of offense. "Take care that this right of yours does not somehow become a stumbling block to the weak,"[12] Paul wrote. He was willing to give up meat, a right he fiercely defended, to avoid offending a brother.

Jesus and Paul were warning against something bigger than the temptation to sin. They were warning about the way in which we set the trap of offense against our own brothers and sisters, our own children. We set ourselves up as models to imitate. We awaken insecurity and offer the wrong solutions. We draw people away from Jesus. The trap of offense forms even in our religion and becomes a barrier to hearing the real words of Christ.

For the mature Christian, offense becomes a question of stewardship. The call to steward Christ's offense is one of the believer's chief concerns and was made so by Jesus himself with a grave warning. As he reminded his disciples the night he was betrayed, their world would be full of offense, but they must not be offended by him or make themselves an offense to others.

Why did Jesus make this warning with such dramatic language, gouging out one's own eye and removing one's own hand if need be? Jesus knew how easily we are drawn into the offense. He knew how quickly our hearts can overcome his offense and then set ourselves up as an offense to others. That is, Jesus knew that we are prone to creating obstacles. Prone to offend out of our pride. Prone to accept his grace and deny it to others. We are prone to reset the very trap we are rescued from. Evangelist D. L. Moody admitted, "Many a professing Christian is a stumbling block because his worship is divided. On Sunday he worships God; on weekdays God has little or no place in his thoughts."[13]

We are called to be extremely careful about giving any offense which is not Christ himself. Jesus was not opposed to offending, but the only thing for which he was willing to risk offense was his good news and the message of the cross itself.

Jesus was clear that we are responsible for the obstacles we place in the path of others. We are called to be stewards of the offense of Christ. That offense must never be us. It must never be offense for the sake of our own rights. We must not offend to protect ourselves or simply to win arguments. Kierkegaard called these "nonessential offense."[14] We risk offense only when it is for the revelation of Christ. We turn the other cheek when struck, bless those who curse, love those who persecute, and sacrifice what we possess so that when we proclaim Christ crucified, it is the offense of the cross alone laid down as an obstacle.

This is the careful work of stewardship that the church, and many of today's believers, have too often neglected. Stewardship requires a keen eye for more than one risk. Many offend to protect themselves and out of their own insecurity. They offend to prove a point or provoke reactions from our culture. But just as many believers have decided never to offend and so have refused to speak the full truth of Christ and his word. They have softened Christ's message and have robbed it of its power to change hearts and expose the trap. We have ended up with two churches: one that so often offends its message is never heard and the other so reluctant to offend it has no message left. What we need are those who have themselves seen the value of Christ's offense and by it have been freed to sacrifice all in the name of stewarding the offense of Christ and his cross alone.

HE WHO WIELDS THE SWORD

Japanese culture has an old tradition of sword making, one for which its greatest philosophers and writers have given their attention. As is often true of Japanese craftsmen, the sword maker pursues a perfection for which they must give nearly all their life and attention. Consider this old Japanese story about two craftsmen—one a master, the other his pupil—and their competition to produce the greatest blade.

The pupil, judging himself to have surpassed his teacher's talent, challenged the master craftsman to a competition. They would each produce one sword and test them to see who could produce the finer blade. Both poured themselves into the work and produced remarkable swords. To test them, they agreed to suspend the blades in a nearby stream, the cutting edges facing upstream. The pupil first placed his sword in the water. The sword cut everything that passed by it: insects, leaves, even fish. So sharp was the blade that the wind was split by its edge. All were impressed.

Next, the master placed his blade in the water. Only the leaves were cut. The fish swam right up to the blade and passed by unharmed.

The air hissed as it impacted the blade's edge. The pupil began to taunt his teacher. By all appearances, the master had lost. No one could dispute what they saw. Both men withdrew their swords and placed them back in their sheaths. Hearing the heckling student, a passing monk stepped forward and explained what he had seen. "The first of the swords was by all accounts a fine sword, however, it is a blood-thirsty, evil blade, as it does not discriminate as to who or what it will cut. The second was by far the finer of the two, as it does not needlessly cut that which is innocent and undeserving."[15]

Both craftsmen could construct fine swords. There was no question about their skills. Both could put a fine edge on any blade. But only one of them was truly a master. He was a master not by his technique alone nor by the edge he could produce. He was a master because he possessed the wisdom to know what a sword was for. The teacher possessed a greater wisdom.

Make no mistake: the word of Christ is a blade. A blade sharp enough to cut and divide. Perhaps one of its greatest risks is those who try to wield it without first acquiring the wisdom needed to understand it. How do you acquire such wisdom? The last person prepared to wield the offense of Christ is the person who has not faced it themselves. He who wields Christ's sword must first be cut by it before he is ready to raise it to another.

I wanted this book to be about the world. I wanted it to be about a culture so prone to offense. I wanted it to be about what others had done and how they had diminished the difficult truths of Christ. Sure, those things made it into this book, but to reach the end and think this has been about anyone but yourself is to place a sword in your hand that you do not possess the wisdom to use. This book is about what I have found in my own heart. Hopefully, it has uncovered things in yours as well.

I did not write this book to offend you, but I hope you have encountered the true obstacle of Christ's offense. My prayer is that you will overcome it. My prayer is that by his hard words, your life will be laid bare, your heart cut deep, and your truest needs exposed. I hope you can see the trap you are standing in. I hope you can recognize your insecurity, your idolatry, your imitation, and the good news that offers you a better affirmation and a way out of the accusation.

Does it hurt? Sure. Would it be easier to ignore it? Perhaps in the short term. But it is through this pain, the exposing of your soul, that Christ works his greatest change.

One of my favorite poets was twentieth-century writer T. S. Eliot. He converted to the Christian faith later in life. Out of that conversation, he wrote one of the greatest poems in English literature, *Four Quartets*. At the center of that poem is Eliot's description of his own healing and the pain by which it came.

> Beneath the bleeding hands we feel
> The sharp compassion of the healer's art
> Resolving the enigma of the fever chart

The bleeding hands Eliot depicts are those of Christ, who works his healing with a "sharp compassion." That work is the only way of understanding the fever which plagues us all.

> Our only health is the disease
> If we obey the dying nurse
> Whose constant care is not to please
> But to remind of our, and Adam's curse,
> And that, to be restored, our sickness must grow worse.[16]

To be restored, our sickness must grow worse. It is all there. To be healed, we must first be made to see that we are sick. To find grace, we must encounter hard truths. To have Christ, we must be prepared to die to ourselves. But do not mistake Christ's hard words, his offense, for anything other than what it is: good news, the best news, the news by which all things are forever changed and healed.

Receive the hard words of Christ and be changed by them.

* * *

"Blessed is the one who is not offended by me." — Matthew 11:6

ACKNOWLEDGMENTS

I owe the biggest thanks to my wife for her faithful help in all my writing and life. A book represents years of work, and it's your steadfast support that helps me see it through. To write well, one must first live well, and you help me do that better every day.

To Pastor Alan Baker, I owe you thanks for your wise and faithful counsel. Our bi-weekly calls have helped me learn to recognize my own insecurities and idols all too well. You've often been willing to be the voice of Christ's hard words that I've needed. Every pastor needs a pastor, and I am blessed to have you in my life. To Janet Grant, who has offered steadfast and wise counsel at every step of this endeavor. I'm grateful for your consistent belief in the work I'm doing.

I owe more thanks to a great team of editors who have helped shape this book: Andrew Spencer, Paul Smith, and Blake Atwood. It is a gift to work with such wise and thoughtful editors.

And to the men and women of Bent Oak Church, I am and will always be your pastor first. So many of these ideas have formed in our congregational life together. Your love of scripture and your constant encouragement make me a better pastor and writer. I'm forever grateful for your humility and interest in exploring Jesus's hard words. I am grateful God us brought us all together.

NOTES

CHAPTER 1: HARD WORDS TO HEAR

1. C.S. Lewis, *The Screw Tape Letters* (New York: HarperOne, 1996), 15.

2. Edward Bernays, *Propaganda* (New York: Ig Publishing, 1955), 74.

3. Genesis 4:7.

4. C. S. Lewis, "Answers to Questions on Christianity," in *God in the Dock* (Grand Rapids: Eerdmans, 1970), 52.

5. C. S. Lewis, *Letters of C. S. Lewis*, ed. Walter Hooper (Boston: Mariner Books, 1988), 426–427.

6. C. S Lewis, *The Screwtape Letters* (New York: HarperOne, 1966), 170.

7. C. S Lewis, *The Screwtape Letters*, 10.

8. Jeremiah 17:9–10.

9. J. Baxter Oliphant, "For many Americans, views of offensive speech aren't necessarily clear-cut," Pew Research Center, December 14, 2021, https://pewresearch.org/fact-tank/2021/12/14/for-many-americans-views-of-offensive-speech-arent-necessarily-clear-cut/.

10. "I'm Offended" Google Books Ngram Viewer, accessed November 25, 2022, https://books.google.com/ngrams/graph?content=I%27m+offended&year_start=1800&year_end=2019&corpus=26&smoothing=3.

11. Rebecca Nicholson, "'Poor little snowflake' – the defining insult of 2016," The Guardian, November 28, 2016, https://theguardian.com/science/2016/nov/28/snowflake-insult-disdain-young-people.

12. Tim Kreider, *We Learn Nothing: Essays and Cartoons* (New York: Simon & Schuster, 2013), 51.

13. René Girard, *I See Satan Fall Like Lightning*, trans. James G. Williams (Maryknoll, NY: Orbis Books, 2001), 16.

14. Luke 17:1, NKJV.

15. Charles Wesley, "Gentle Jesus, Meek and Mild [A Child's Prayer]" Hymns & Sacred Poems, 1742, Hymnary.org, accessed April 9, 2024, https://hymnary.org/text/gentle_jesus_meek_and_mild_look_upon.

16. Matthew 11:6, NKJV.

17. David McCracken, *The Scandal of the Gospels*, 22.

18. See 1 Corinthians 8:9 and 1 Peter 2:8.

19. David McCracken, *The Scandal of the Gospels*, 64.

20. Gilbert Keith Chesterton, *Orthodoxy* (New York: John Lane Company, 1908), 32.

21. Søren Kierkegaard, *Training in Christianity and the Edifying Discourses* Which "Accompanied" It, trans. Walter Lowrie (Princeton, NJ: Princeton University Press, 2015), 139.

22. Hebrews 4:12.

23. Revelation 1:16.

24. Luke 2:34–35, NIV.

25. C. S. Lewis, *The Collected Letters of C.S. Lewis*, Volume 3: Narnia, Cambridge, and Joy, 1950–1963, ed. Walter Hooper (New York: HarperCollins, 2007), 606.

26. T. S. Eliot, *Four Quartets* IV, 27.

CHAPTER 2: OFFENSE: "GET BEHIND ME, SATAN!"

1. Franz Kafka, "Reflections on Sin, Pain, Hope, and the True Way," Genius, no. 1, accessed April 9, 2024, https://genius.com/Franz-kafka-reflections-on-sin-pain-hope-and-the-true-way-annotated.

2. Matthew 16:13, NKJV.

3. Matthew 16:15.

4. Matthew 16:16.

5 Matthew 16:17.

6. Matthew 16:22, paraphrased.

7. Matthew 16:23, NIV.

8. Simone Weil, "Evil," in *The Simone Weil Reader* (New York: Moyer Bell

Ltd., 2007), 383.

9. Flannery O'Connor, "The Fiction Writer & His Country," in *Mystery and Manners Occasional Prose*, eds. Sally and Robert Fitzgerald (New York: Farrar, Straus and Giroux, 1969), 34.

10. Craig S. Keener, *The Gospel of Matthew: A Socio-Rhetorical Commentary* (Grand Rapids: Eerdmans, 2009) 150.

11. Matthew 4:19.

12. John 1:42.

13. Matthew 4:9, author's paraphrase.

14. Psalm 91:12.

15. Proverbs 3:23.

16. The Greek word for salvation, σωτηρία, is used forty-three times in the New Testament while the Greek noun, σκάνδαλον, is used fifteen times and the Greek verb, σκανδαλίζω, is used thirty times.

17. David McCracken, *The Scandal of the Gospels*, 8.

18. René Girard, *I See Satan Fall Like Lightning*, 17.

19. David McCracken, *The Scandal of the Gospels*, 6.

20. Gil Bailie, "Scandal and Imitation," *Contagion: Journal of Violence, Mimesis, and Culture*, Volumes 3–4 (1996): 148.

21. Leviticus 19:14.

22. Yehoshua Karsh, "Lifnei Ivver," Sefaria, accessed November 25, 2022, https://www.sefaria.org/sheets/77834?lang=bi.

23. Robert G. Hamerton-Kelly, *The Gospel and the Sacred: Poetics of Violence in Mark* (Minneapolis, MN: Fortress, 1993), 40.

24. Isaiah 8:13–14, NET.

25. Winn Collier, *A Burning In My Bones: The Authorized Biography of Eugene H. Peterson, Translator of The Message* (Colorado Springs, CO: Water-Brook, 2021), 38–39.

26. Winn Collier, *A Burning In My Bones*, 39.

27. Matthew 15:14.

28. John 9:39.

29. Dietrich Bonhoeffer, *Life Together* (New York: Harper & Row Publishers, Inc., 1954), 99.

30. 1 Peter 2:4–8.

31. Dante Alighieri, *The Divine Comedy: Inferno; Purgatorio; Paradiso*, trans.

Allen Mandelbaum (New York: Everyman's Library Classics, 1995).

CHAPTER 3: INSECURITY: "WHY DO YOU CALL ME GOOD?"

1. Mark 10:17.
2. Mark 10:18.
3. Dietrich Bonhoeffer, *The Cost of Discipleship*, trans. Chr. Kaiser Verlag München, R. H. Fuller, and Irmgard Booth (New York: Touchstone, 1995), 71.
4. Mark 10:21.
5. Alan Watts, *The Wisdom of Insecurity: A Message for an Age of Anxiety* (New York: Vintage Books, 1979), 76–77.
6. Mark 10:20, author's paraphrase..
7. Mark Whitehouse, "Number of the Week: Americans Buy More Stuff They Don't Need," *The Wall Street Journal*, April 23, 2011, https://www. wsj.com/articles/BL-REB-13793; Mary MacVeen, "For many people, gathering possessions is just the stuff of life," LA Times, March 21, 2014, https://www.latimes.com/health/la-xpm-2014-mar-21-la-he-keeping-stuff-20140322-story.html.
8. Shirley M. Mueller M.D., "Collecting: Beyond Freud and Muensterberger," *Psychology Today*, May 24, 2022, https://www.psychologytoday.com/us/blog/the-mind-collector/202205/collecting-beyond-freud-and-muensterberger.
9. C. S. Lewis, *Mere Christianity* (New York: HarperOne, 1952), 122.
10. Sigmund Freud, *New Introductory Lectures on Psycho-Analysis* (New York: W. W. Norton & Company, 1989), 208.
11. Alan Watts, *The Wisdom of Insecurity* (New York: Vintage Books, 2011), 14–15.
12. Bonhoeffer, *Cost of Discipleship*, 72.
13. Bonhoeffer, *Cost of Discipleship*, 72.
14. Genesis 2:25.
15. Genesis 3:1.
16. Leon R. Kass, *The Beginning of Wisdom: Reading Genesis* (New York: Free Press, 2003), 83.
17. Genesis 3:5.
18. Genesis 3:6.
19. Isabella Poggi and Francesca D'Errico, "Feeling Offended: A Blow to Our

Image and Our Social Relationships," *Frontiers in Psychology*, Volume 8, 17 January 2018, 4, https://www.frontiersin.org/journals/psychology/articles/10.3389/fpsyg.2017.02221/full.

20. Isabella Poggi and Francesca D'Errico, "Feeling Offended," 14.

21. Matthew 19:18–19.

22. Matthew 19:20.

23. Matthew 19:25–26.

24. Matthew 5:3–10.

25. See Matthew 18:2–4.

26. Matthew 19:21, author's paraphrase.

27. Friedrich Nietzsche, *The Gay Science*, trans. Walter Kaufmann (New York: Vintage Publishing, 1974), 181–82.

28. Friedrich Nietzsche, *The Gay Science*, 181.

29. Friedrich Nietzsche, *The Gay Science*, 181.

30. Friedrich Nietzsche, *The Gay Science*, 182.

31. René Girard, *Evolution and Conversion: Dialogues on the Origins of Culture* (New York: Bloomsbury Academic, 2008), 159.

32. David Foster Wallace, *This Is Water: Some Thoughts Delivered in a Significant Occasion about Living a Compassionate Life* (New York: Little, Brown and Company, 2009), 101.

CHAPTER 4: OBSESSION: "YOU HYPOCRITES!"

1. Matthew 15:2.

2. Matthew 15:7–9.

3. Isaiah 29:14.

4. Matthew 15:12.

5. Moshe Halbertal and Avishai Margalit, *Idolatry*, trans. Naomi Goldblum (Cambridge, MA: Harvard University Press, 1992), 8.

6. G. K. Beale, *We Become What We Worship: A Biblical Theology of Idolatry* (Downers Grove, IL: IVP Academic, 2008), 169.

7. Luke 18:9–14.

8. Luke 18:13.

9. Matthew 23:27–28.

10. G. K. Beale, *We Become What We Worship*, 17.

11. Richard Lints, *Identity and Idolatry: The Image of God and Its Inversion* (Downers Grove, IL: InterVarsity Press, 2015), 87.

12. Richard Lints, *Identity and Idolatry*, 86.

13. Romans 1:22–23.

14. Exodus 32:1–6.

15. Joshua J. Mark, "Egyptian Gods—The Complete List," *World History Encyclopedia*, April 14, 2016, https://worldhistory.org/article/885/egyptian-gods---the-complete-list/.

16. Exodus 32:4.

17. Ezekiel 14:3.

18. *The Cambridge Companion to John Calvin*, ed. Donald K. McKim (Cambridge, Cambridge University Press, 2004), 85.

19. Timothy Keller, *Counterfeit Gods: The Empty Promises of Money, Sex, and Power, and the Only Hope that Matters* (New York: Penguin Books, 2009), 168.

20. Joseph Joubert, *The Notebooks of Joseph Joubert*, trans. Paul Auster (New York: New York Review of Books, 1983), 24.

21. C. S. Lewis, *The Collected Letters of C. S. Lewis*, Volume 3 (New York: HarperCollins, 2004), 759.

22. Marcel Proust, *In Search of Lost Time*, Volume V, The Captive; the Fugitive, rev. ed., trans. C. K. Scott Moncrieff and Terence Kilmartin (New York: The Modern Library, 2003), 628.

23. Charlotte Brontë, *Jane Eyre* (New York, Penguin Books, 1847), 35.

24. Charlotte Brontë, *Jane Eyre*, 82.

25. G. K. Chesterton in Karen Swallow Prior, Charlotte Brontë, *Jane Eyre: A Guide to Reading and Reflecting* (Nashville: B&H Publishing Group, 2021), 15.

26. Charlotte Brontë, *Jane Eyre*, 316.

27 Graham Greene, *The End of the Affair* (New York: Penguin Books, 1979), 55.

28. Genesis 3:5.

29. Genesis 3:6.

30. René Girard, *Battling to the End* (East Lansing, MI: Michigan State University Press, 2010), 112.

31. Thomas Chalmers (1780–1847), *The Expulsion of a New Affection* (Wheaton, IL: Crossway, 2020), 36.

32. Charles Taylor, *A Secular Age* (Cambridge, MA: The Belknap Press, 2007), 299.

33. The Dis, "Happily Ever After Magic Kingdom Fireworks 4K Full Show + Outro | Walt Disney World," May 12, 2017, 00:25 to 00:49 and 04:31 to 04:36, https://www.youtube.com/watch?v=d7FFFENv6i4.

34. Faye Fiore, "America as Disney's Land: The Fantasy vs. the Reality: Culture: A nation mirrored by the company's creations re-examines the image reflected in its corporate agenda," *Los Angeles Times*, September 25, 1994, https://www.latimes.com/archives/la-xpm-1994-09-25-mn-42972-story.html.

35. Charles Taylor, *The Ethics of Authenticity* (Cambridge, MA: Harvard University Press, 1991): 14.

36. Charles Taylor, *The Ethics of Authenticity*, 27.

37. Matthew 4:4.

38. "The End of Absolutes: America's New Moral Code," *Barna*, May 25, 2016, https://www.barna.com/research/the-end-of-absolutes-americas-new-moral-code/.

39. "The End of Absolutes: America's New Moral Code," *Barna*.

40. Robert Bellah, et al, Habits of the Heart: Individualism and Commitment in *American Life* (Berkley, CA: University of California Press, 1996), 142.

CHAPTER 5: IMITATION: "WHO ARE YOU TO ASK ME?"

1. René Girard, *I See Satan Fall Like Lightning*, 32–33.

2. John 4:5.

3. John 4:9.

4. Craig S. Keener, *The Gospel of John: A Commentary*, Vol. 1 (Grand Rapids, MI: Baker Academic, 2003), 598.

5. John 4:10.

6. John 4:10.

7. Leon Morris, *The Gospel According to John*, Rev. ed. (Grand Rapids, MI: Wm. B. Eerdmans, Co., 1995), 227.

8. Craig S. Keener, *The Gospel of John*, 596.

9. John 4:25–26.

10. Craig S. Keener, *The Gospel of John*, 584.

11. John 3:2.

12. John 3:3.

13. Dietrich Bonhoeffer, *The Cost of Discipleship*, 94.

14. Galatians 3:28.

15. Isaiah 6:5.

16. René Girard, *Oedipus Unbound: Selected Writings on Rivalry and Desire* (Stanford, CA: Stanford University Press, 2004), xxxiii.

17. Walter Burkert, René Girard, and Jonathan Smith, "Generative Scapegoating," *Violent Origins* (Stanford, CA: Stanford University Press, 1987), 122.

18. René Girard, Deceit, *Desire & The Novel: Self and Other Literary Structure*, trans. Yvonne Freccero (Baltimore, MD: The John Hopkins University Press, 1965), 15.

19. Georg Christoph Lichtenberg, *The Waste Books*, trans. R. J. Hollingdale (New York: New York Review of Books, 2000), 59.

20. Chris Palmer, "How to Overcome Imposter Phenomenon," *Monitor on Psychology*, Vol. 52 No. 4, (2021), 44.

21. Luke Burgis, *Wanting: The Power of Mimetic Desire in Everyday Life* (New York: St. Martin's Publishing Group, 2021), 21.

22. Luke Burgis, *Wanting: The Power of Mimetic*, 22.

23. Neil Postman, *Amusing Ourselves to Death: Public Discourse in the Age of Show Business* (New York: Penguin Books, 1985), 128.

24. Rudie Le Roux, "Unforgettable Commercial Stelvio Alfa Romeo USA," July 21, 2018, https://www.youtube.com/watch?v=vQwDXlrL9bM.

25. John 4:29, author's paraphrase.

26. Matthew 16:24–25.

CHAPTER 6: AFFIRMATION: "WOMAN, WHAT IS IT TO ME?"

1. C. S. Lewis, *The Screwtape Letters* (New York: HarperOne, 1966), 80–81.

2. John 2:3.

3. Craig S. Keener, *The Gospel of John*, 503.

4. John 2:4.

5. Luke 2:48.

6. Luke 2:49.

7. Luke 2:51.

8. Van Wyck Broos, *Writers at Work: The Paris Review Interviews*, Second Series (New York: Viking Press, 1966), 368.

9. Craig S. Keener, *The Gospel of John,* 506.

10. John 2:4.

11. Leon Morris, *The Gospel According to John*, 158.

12. Craig S. Keener, *The Gospel of John*, 505.

13. John 2:4.

14. Mark 5:7.

15. Luke 14:26.

16. Matthew 12:48–50.

17. Isaiah 30:10.

18. St Augustine, *Saint Augustine's Anti-Pelagian Works* (Woodstock, Canada: Devoted Publishing, 2017), 525–526.

19. 2 Timothy 4:2–3, NIV.

20. Neil Postman, *Amusing Ourselves to Death*, xxi.

21. Philip Rieff, *The Triumph of the Therapeutic: Uses of Faith after Freud* (Chicago, IL: University of Chicago Press, 1987), 25.

22. Christopher Lasch, *The Culture of Narcissism: American Life in an Age of Diminishing Expectations* (New York: W. W. Norton & Company, 1979), 7–8.

23. Alasdair MacIntyre, *After Virtue: A Study in Moral Theology* (London: Bloomsbury Academic, 2007), 13.

24. Eugene H. Peterson, *A Long Obedience in the Same Direction: Discipleship in an Instant Society* (Downers Grove, IL: IVP Books, 2000), 48.

25. Rieff, *The Triumph of the Therapeutic*, 26.

26. Carl Trueman, "Christianity, Liberalism and the New Evangelicalism," *The Theologian*, http://www.theologian.org.uk/doctrine/liberalism.html.

27. Carl Trueman, "Divine Therapy," *Touchstone*, https://www.touchstonemag.com/archives/article.php?id=34-05-020-v.

28. Alexandra Sifferlin, "Study Reveals Americans' Contradictory Thoughts on Self-Improvement," *Time Magazine*, December 1, 2014, https://time.com/3612360/americans-self-improvement-survey/.

29. "Buddy Christ," Wikipedia, https://en.wikipedia.org/wiki/Buddy_Christ.

30. Timothy Keller, @tinkellernyc, "Post text," Twitter, September 12, 2014, 11 am, https://twitter.com/timkellernyc/status/510458013606739968?lang=en.

31. Luke 11:27–28.

32. Augustine quoted in *Ancient Christian Commentary on Scripture*, New Testament III, Luke, ed. Thomas C. Oden (Grand Rapids, IL: IVP Academic, 2003), 195.

33. John 2:5.

34. Rodney A. Whitacre, *John*, The IVP New Testament Commentary Series, series ed., Grant B. Osborne (Downers Grove, IL: IVP Academic, 1999), 80.

35. C. S. Lewis, *Mere Christianity*, 227.

CHAPTER 7: ACCUSATION: "TOSS IT TO THE DOGS"

1. C. G. Jung, *Collected Works of C. G. Jung*, 225.

2. George H. Guthrie, *Commentary on the New Testament Use of the Old Testament* (Grand Rapids, MI; Baker Academic, 1994), 54.

3. Matthew 15:22.

4. Matthew 15:24–25.

5. Matthew 15:26.

6. Matthew 15:27.

7. Proverbs 26:11; 1 Samuel 17:43; 2 Kings 9:10; Luke 16:21; Philippians 3:2; Revelation 22:15.

8. Matthew 15:8. See Isaiah 29:13.

9. Matthew 15:12.

10. Matthew 15:13, 16.

11. Matthew 13:21.

12. Simone G. Shamay-Tsoory, Dorin Ahronberg-Kirschenbaum, and Nirit Bauminger-Zviely, "There Is No Joy like Malicious Joy: Schadenfreude in Young Children," *PLOS ONE*, July 2, 2014, https://journals.plos.org/plosone/article?id=10.1371/journal.pone.0100233.

13. Shamay-Tsoory, Ahronberg-Kirschenbaum, and Bauminger-Zviely, "There Is No Joy like Malicious Joy."

14. Shamay-Tsoory, Ahronberg-Kirschenbaum, and Bauminger-Zviely, "There Is No Joy like Malicious Joy."

15. René Girard, "Are the Gospels Mythical," *First Things*, April 1996, https://www.firstthings.com/article/1996/04/are-the-gospels-mythical.

16. Fyodor Dostoyevsky, *Notes from the Underground*, trans. Richard Pevear and Larissa Volokbonsky (New York: Vintage Books, 1994), 50.

17. Fyodor Dostoevsky, *The Brothers Karamazov*, trans. Richard Pevear and Larissa Volokhonsky (New York: Borzoi Book, 1992), 44.

18. Genesis 3:11, NET.

19. Genesis 3:12.

20. Genesis 3:13.

21. Matthew 7:3-5.

22. Aleksandr I. Solzhenitsyn, *The Gulag Archipelago 1918–1956: An Experiment in Literary Investigation*, trans. Thomas P. Whitney (New York: Harper & Row, Publishers, 1974), 168.

23. John 8:7. Author's paraphrase.

24. Jeremiah 17:13.

25. Jeremiah 17:9–10.

26. John 8:11, KJV.

27. René Girard, *I See Satan Fall Like Lightning*, 164.

28. René Girard, *I See Satan Fall Like Lightning*, 165.

29. Romans 3:15–17; see Isaiah 59:7–8.

30. Romans 3:10.

31. Job 1:9–10, author's paraphrase.

32. Job 2:9, author's paraphrase.

33. René Girard, *I Saw Satan Fall Like Lightning*, 33.

34. See Genesis 11:1–9.

35. David McCracken, *The Scandal of the Gospels,* 19.

36. Sam Storms, "The Faith of a 'Dog,'" *Enjoying God*, April 27, 2015, .

CHAPTER 8: HEALING: "YOU WILL BE OFFENDED BY ME"

1. Eugene Peterson, *Living the Resurrection: The Risen Christ in Everyday Life* (Colorado Springs, CO: NavPress, 2006), 96.

2. Martin Hengel, *Crucifixion in the Ancient World and the Folly of the Message of the Cross*, trans. John Bowden (Philadelphia, PA: Fortress Press, 1977), 42.

3. Matthew 26:31, author's translation.

4. Matthew 26:31; see Zechariah 13:7.

5. Matthew 26:33, author's translation.

6. Matthew 26:34.

7. John 16:1–4.

8. Søren Kierkegaard, *Practice in Christianity*, eds. and trans. Howard V. Hong and Edna H. Hong (Princeton, NJ: Princeton University Press, 1991), 237.

9. Eric Hoffer, *The Passionate State of Mind, and Other Aphorisms* (New York: Harper, 1955), 21.

10. René Girard, *I See Satan Fall Like Lightning*, 13.

11. Gilbert Keith Chesterton, *The Collected Works of G.K. Chesterton*, Volume 29 (San Francisco, CA: Ignatius Press, 1986), 148.

12. L. Nelson Bell, "The Offense of the Cross," *Christianity Today*, April 25, 1960, https://www.christianitytoday.com/ct/1960/april-25/layman-and-his-faith.html.

13. 1 Corinthians 2:1–2.

14. 1 Corinthians 1:22–23.

15. C. S. Lewis, *Mere Christianity*, 193.

16. John 11:50.

17. René Girard, *The Girard Reader*, ed. James G. Williams (Chestnut Ridge, PA: Crossroad Publishing Company, 1996), 200.

18. 1 Peter 2:23.

19. Matthew 26:39.

20. Luke 23:34.

21. John Stott, *The Cross of Christ* (Downers Grove, IL: InterVarsity Press, 1986), 334.

22. C. S. Lewis, *The Voyage of the Dawn Treader* (New York: MacMillan Publishing Co., Inc., 1952), 89–90.

23. Jerry Bridges, *Transforming Grace* (Colorado Springs, CO: NavPress, 1991), 39.

24. David McCracken, *The Scandal of the Gospels,* 9.

25. John 21:15.

26. John 21:15, author's paraphrase.

27. John 21:15–17.

28. 1 Peter 2:4–8.

CHAPTER 9: SHOULD WE TOO OFFEND?

1. William Hazlitt, *Characteristics: in the manner of Rochefoucault's Maxims* (London: J. Templeton, 1937), 139.

2. Quoted in, David McCracken, *The Scandal of the Gospels*, 66.

3. John 17:1, author's paraphrase.

4. John 17:1.

5. Matthew 17:24.

6. Matthew 17:25.

7. Matthew 17:25.

8. Matthew 17:26.

9. Matthew 17:27.

10. Nicholas Thomas Wright, *Matthew for Everyone*, Part 2: Chapters 16–28 (Louisville, KY: Westminster Knox Press, 2002), 17.

11. Matthew 18:8, KJV.

12. 1 Corinthians 8:9.

13. Dwight L. Moody, *D. L. Moody on the Ten Commandments* (Chicago: Moody Press, 1977), 22.

14. Quoted in, David McCracken, *The Scandal of the Gospels*, 118.

15. Markus Sesko, *Masamune—His Work, His fame and His Legacy* (Morrisville, NC: Lulu Press, Inc., 2014), 74.

16. T. S. Eliot, *Four Quartets* (London: Faber & Faber, 2019), 27.